DOMINIC LITTLEWOOD

Dom was born in Southend in 1965. His family had a strong work ethic. His mum and dad both had two jobs. He says he got his sense of humour from his dad and his business acumen from his mum. He has no time for moaners. When things go wrong his attitude is 'the milk has been split, now just get on with it!'

His strength of character was put to the test in 1990 when he broke his neck in an accident. Doctors told him he was lucky not to be paralysed for life. After making a full recovery, this inspired him to concentrate on knuckling down and becoming successful.

Dom has always lived on his wits. He started in car sales as a teenager and built a reputation as an outstanding salesman in a highly competitive world. 'You have to be good to survive. If you miss an opportunity, someone else will grab it. Don't miss that moment.'

Dom's life changed in 2000, when he appeared as a contestant on a TV quiz show. He enjoyed some quick-fire banter with the show's host, Dale Winton. TV executives were quick to see Dom's natural talent and he was soon appearing on Channel 4's *Faking It*, teaching a vicar how to be a successful salesperson in just one month. Other TV offers followed and Dom made the most of the opportunity and has been a regular on TV screens ever since.

'I've always felt at ea[illegible]
don't try too hard. You c[illegible]
try to be myself and act [illegible]

Dom has starred in [illegible]
Dancing and *The One Sho*[illegible]
his very best. He faces every challenge with steely determination and, when the time is right, a cheeky sense of humour. He shows viewers how to stay cool under pressure, whether they are chasing a bargain, a refund or a victory over red tape.

'Don't let yourself be short-changed.' This is Dom's view of life. His positive attitude can work for you too. This book shows you how . . .

Don't Get Done, Get Dom

How to stretch your money, not your budget

Dominic Littlewood

with Tony Norman

First published in 2009 by
HEADLINE PUBLISHING GROUP

1

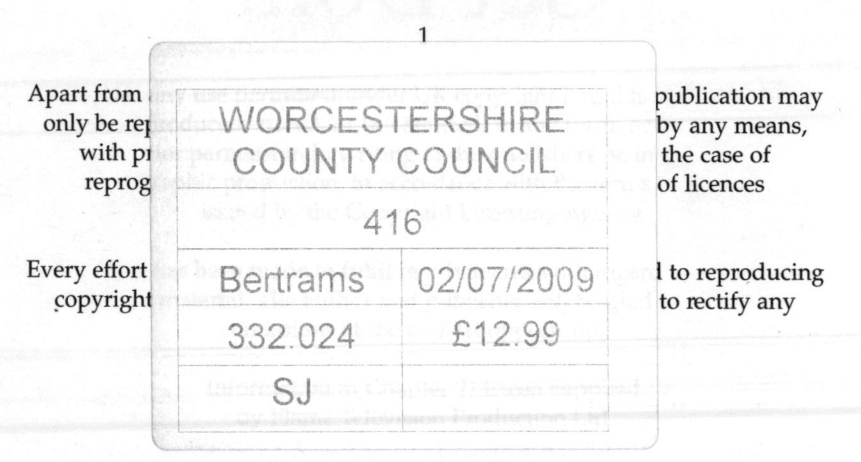

Cataloguing in Publication Data is available from the British Library

ISBN 978 0 7553 1945 9

Typeset in Palatino by Avon DataSet Ltd,
Bidford-on-Avon, Warwickshire

Printed and bound in Great Britain by
Clays Ltd, St Ives plc

Headline's policy is to use papers that are natural, renewable and recyclable products and made from wood grown in sustainable forests. The logging and manufacturing processes are expected to conform to the environmental regulations of the country of origin.

HEADLINE PUBLISHING GROUP
An Hachette UK Company
338 Euston Road
London NW1 3BH

www.headline.co.uk
www.hachette.co.uk

CONTENTS

PREFACE

This book could save you hundreds or even thousands of pounds in the current credit crunch.

If, like millions of other shoppers, you have never dreamed of haggling with sales staff for the bargain of a lifetime, Dominic Littlewood will show you how. Prepare to be dazzled!

In BBC One's hit series *Don't Get Done, Get Dom,* the likeable presenter became a consumer crusader. As well as showing viewers how to make amazing savings on the high street, Dom also battles against bureaucracy. It is easy to feel powerless when faced with a huge organisation. How do you get your money back when you have been short-changed? How do you get justice when you feel your rights have been trampled upon?

The answers are all here in the official *Don't Get Done, Get Dom* book.

Learn how to beat the recession and fight back against red tape.

See how Dom's top tips can make your money go further than you ever thought possible.

Welcome to the rest of your life!

INTRODUCTION

'Let the people's champion Dominic Littlewood bag you a bargain or help you battle bureaucracy!'

With these bold words, BBC One launched its brand new consumer affairs programme, *Don't Get Done, Get Dom*, back in 2006. Right from the start, the show was a winner. Viewers related to Dom in a big way. They liked the positive way he dealt with every problem he faced.

Suddenly, viewers saw it was possible to stand up for themselves by following Dom's crystal clear guidelines. They were inspired by his strong personality and determination to succeed. Viewers realised this was a show you could really learn from. Word spread and soon *Don't Get Done, Get Dom* was attracting a large regular audience.

Three series have now been made by Flame Television Production Ltd. A total of sixty 45-minute shows. Every programme is full of excellent consumer advice and the timing is spot on. With the credit crunch biting hard, people all over Britain are watching every penny they spend. We need help more now than ever before. This book features the best tips and tricks from all three series. Learn how to get the best value for money every time. Stand up for your rights and get the fair treatment you deserve.

We are living in a tough world and it's getting harder every day. Dom's advice is clear, well-informed and easy to follow. With his warm, common sense approach, Dom is the perfect person to guide you through the current downturn. His eternal optimism will encourage you to deal successfully with salespeople and bureaucrats alike.

Be a winner . . . *Don't Get Done, Get Dom!*

DO IT LIKE DOM

Dominic Littlewood says *everything* is possible

I love haggling!

I was born that way. Even as a little boy, I didn't like taking no for an answer when it came to getting a deal. In *Don't Get Done, Get Dom* I show how being positive can really change your life . . . and your wallet. This book features the best tips and tricks from the first three series. Learn how to get the best value for money every time. Stand up for your rights and get the fair treatment you deserve.

Want to know how to get the best deal on the high street? No problem, I'll show you how.

Angry about not getting a refund for shoddy goods or services? No worries. We can deal with that.

Worn down by the frustration of dealing with red tape on a community issue that really matters to you? I can help there too.

In every case my advice is the same.

Stay calm. Stay focused. Use the tips I give in *Don't Get Done, Get Dom*.

Why? Because they work!

My first haggle

I was just four when I haggled for the first time. I had an accident on my very first day at school. I tried to jump over a chair, caught my toe and landed on my chin. It was a bad cut and I had to go to hospital for stitches. Both my parents were at work, so the next-door neighbour had to come down. Not who a four-year-old wants to see when he's pouring with blood, and the nurse is trying to come at you with a needle and thread.

As a young child I was very headstrong. I was kicking, screaming, crying, anything I could do. I remember the nurse offering me a toy to pacify me and I didn't like it, it didn't work. I had my eye on this huge yellow dumper truck. It wasn't necessarily a better toy, but it wasn't offered to me, so there was a challenge immediately. I just kept pointing at the truck, that's what I want, that's what I want. And finally, when it was put in my hands, I laid down, kept quiet and took my stitches like the brave little soldier I was.

I can remember it all very clearly and thinking I'd got something I shouldn't have got just by asking. So I realised at a very early age: ask for more than you expect, even if you don't think you'll get it. Ask anyhow because you might just find you get what you want. That's still my philosophy today.

I'll haggle over anything.

I remember proving that to a friend of mine. This was at the time when it was fashionable for men to wear one earring. He'd seen an earring in a jeweller's for £4.99. I told him I could get a discount on it. I went in with him and got 25 per cent off, £1.25. When we came out he said, *I can't believe that. I wouldn't dare ask for a discount on a £4.99 earring*. I said, *Well, that's the difference between you and me*. It's not the principal, it's the money.

I enjoy shopping. I think a bit of retail therapy does you the world of good. And when I start asking for a discount and get that banter going with the shopkeepers, it makes the whole day that much more fun. I love it and I do it all the time. I've had that spirit in me since I was young. My mum always said 'Never miss an opportunity in life.' It's the best bit of advice I've ever had. That philosophy found its way into *Don't Get Done, Get Dom*.

Origins of the show

The original idea for the show came about when I had lunch with the BBC One controller. She is a really shrewd, lovely lady but suffers no fools. I get on very well with her. I'd been doing a series for BBC Two called *Wrong Car, Right Car* and it was the first time TV had ever been filmed the way we did it. We gave people hidden earpieces and I mentored them while the deal was going on live, in places where the salespeople didn't know they were being filmed. I'd be around the corner in a van.

I couldn't see a video link, but I could hear what was being said and that was the most important thing. I knew what was going on and I could talk to the people I was helping, who were all members of the public who wanted to buy a car. New or used, it didn't matter. We narrowed it down to one new and one used. I talked to them through their earpiece and helped them to haggle. Of the 22 people we worked with, 21 bought cars they were very happy with.

We got some amazing deals. I remember one woman who turned out to be really good at haggling. She pushed so hard the car salesperson turned round and said to her, *There's nothing left to give. Do you want ten pounds out of my pocket to put some petrol in it?* I (still hidden) said, *Say yes, say yes, say yes,* and she hesitated then said, *Yes please.* And the salesperson stood up and took ten pounds out of his pocket and put it on the table. He said, *You've cleaned me out!* And I was outside in the van saying, *Take the ten pounds, take the ten pounds*. It was hilarious. Of course, the salesperson hadn't been cleaned out, it was just part of their humorous banter.

Viewing figures for that show went over three million, which was more than anyone had expected. It was clear that this style of filming really worked. When *Wrong Car, Right Car* finished and I met the BBC controller for lunch, she asked what I fancied doing next. I said I'd shown people how you can get deals on cars, but it's not just cars, you can do it on anything. She said, *Do you mean anything?* And I said, *Anything*. And she said, *Okay, I like it, let's do it,* and we formatted *Don't Get Done, Get Dom* from there.

Bureaucratic nightmares

Something I feel passionate about is how to deal with bureaucratic nightmares and how to get your money back when things go badly wrong. We decided to incorporate this kind of advice into the new shows. We focused on all sorts of cases where ordinary people deserved justice. These kinds of issues really suits my personality. I'm a very headstrong person: extremely stubborn. I will dig my heels in. My dad was the same; he would spend three hundred pounds to argue about a ten pound bill if he felt he was right. He would argue and fight for it tooth and nail and I've got that gene from him.

I have taken three companies to the Small Claims Court myself in the past, because I didn't like what they were doing. I didn't agree with their principles. If something's not right, I will stand my ground and that's the concept we brought to the programme. We said, let's address people's problems. We all have things that go wrong and that we're not happy with. Whether it's bills, bad workmanship, nightmare holidays or the fact that the sole fell off your shoes after three days – it doesn't matter. We're all unhappy with the service we get from time to time and I try to teach people it's a David and Goliath scenario. Let's stand up to the big boys and teach them a lesson. There are lots of ways of doing it.

What we found on *Don't Get Done, Get Dom* was that we had opened up a can of worms. The BBC, my agent and I all got sack loads of emails and registered delivery letters from people requesting my help to sort out their problems. We still get them, all the time. People want to know how to complain, what to do, how to deal with a situation when you're getting fobbed off and when red tape and bureaucracy are standing in the way of getting resolution. Obviously, I can't take on every individual case. I'd need an office block full of helpers to do that. But this book will answer many of the questions people ask.

What I want the public to pick up on is that if you have some dedication, some tenacity, and keep your calm and your cool, you can fight your own battles very successfully. I like the fact I'm teaching people to do that. I don't like it when people think, *I've got a problem, Dom will sort it out.* That's not the case. I need to educate people to sort out their own problems. Stand up for yourself and be persistent. We get that message across in *Don't Get Done, Get Dom.*

Haggling in shops

Teaching people how to haggle in shops is a major part of the show and I get a lot of retailers mocking me and joking with me. Some of them moan but it's never aggressive. They say, *I keep getting people coming and asking for a discount.* I say, *You shouldn't knock me, you should be thanking me for the fact that there are people coming in.* If they ask for a discount and you give it, quite often what you're doing is buying the customer's loyalty.

Retailers with a negative attitude will say, *I don't want people coming in here asking for a discount*. My attitude to that is you have to move with the times. You'll be out of business soon if you don't. These are changing times and customers are looking for the best deals they can get, whether it's on the high street or the internet.

As far as shopkeepers are concerned, profit is not a dirty word. They're entitled to their profit. We all go to work, we all earn our wages. What I'm saying to retailers is, make people feel good about what you're doing by allowing people to haggle. People are shrewd now, they've got to watch their pennies. They will haggle more and that can be a good thing for shops and shoppers. It works both ways.

When Brits are abroad, they love going to markets and haggling. The whole environment is set up like that. Everybody, every stall and every shop is bartering, so they do it too and have some fun. Even the most embarrassed and reserved of Brits will haggle in those places because they feel it's expected, and they enjoy it. They don't really know whether they've bought something at cost price or whether they've paid a fortune for it, but they've enjoyed the experience.

And that's what we should do more in this country now: shake off that old British reserve. The attitude that says, *That's the label price, that's what we've got to pay*. You *can* haggle in the UK. I do it all the time. The advice I give people in *Don't Get Done, Get Dom* is more relevant today in the credit crunch than ever. It's a buyer's market: there's never been a better time to haggle.

My message to retailers is: make your customers feel good. Don't just sell them a product, then wait for the next person to come through the door. Give them such a good deal they go out and tell their friends and family, *Go and see that guy; he's great*. When I say that I'm basing it on my own experiences as a salesperson. That's how they operate in the car industry.

When I was younger I worked for a big g arage in Basildon and I used to get generations of family members coming in to see me because I'd given their brother, sister or parent such good service when I sold them a car. They used to walk into the showroom and there'd be half a dozen salespeople there all chomping at the bit to get their business. But they'd say, *No, we're here to see Dominic*. That used to give me a big buzz and the other salespeople a big wake-up call.

I'd have people queuing up at my desk to speak to me about buying cars, while the other salespeople were sitting around twiddling their thumbs and moaning to the sales manager. They'd say, *He's got four people waiting there, this is not on*. And the sales manager would say, *What's the answer to that? If people want to deal with him, then he's doing something right and you're not*. I used to have that all the time.

The place where I worked was the largest independent garage in Europe. They commissioned a survey into what their customers thought of the sales staff. Now this may sound conceited, but it's not meant to be. I'm just saying I've always believed in a high level of customer care and the survey proved I was on the right track. The customers said, *That Dominic, he's unbelievable. He's the only person I know that I feel I can trust. I've come in to see him with a problem before; he's just dropped everything, sorted it out. He ran me home. He didn't have to do that. He did this, he did that . . .*

The management showed me the report and it couldn't have been better if I'd written it myself. They said, *Whatever you're doing, we wish other people would do it too*. That was twenty years ago and I was on seventy grand a year. Sixty-seven thousand pounds of that was commission. I had directors going mad. I was earning three or four times what they were earning because I was doing what I was good at. Why was I earning that much money? People trusted me, people liked me, I did a good job, I didn't lie, I was always honest, and subsequently it had a knock-on effect. I couldn't go wrong.

Tricks of the trade

I learnt a lot at that time and I used those experiences on *Don't Get Done, Get Dom*. I knew the tricks of the trade when it came to selling, so I could warn people what to look out for. For example, when I was a salesperson I went on a training course, which was quite valuable. It was all about not giving discounts on cars. As a nation, Brits can feel awkward about asking for discount, especially when not on holiday! We don't like doing it, although deep down we know we should. So quite often people won't ask and if they do, they do it in a negative way.

They may say, *I don't suppose you'd do a discount?* Or, *No chance of a discount, is there?* It's said in a negative way and a trained salesperson will easily read the signs. They can see you're not a negotiator, you're not a haggler, and you feel awkward asking for a discount. What they taught me on that course was that as a salesperson, you don't even need to answer the question. Just change the subject and the customer will never ask for a discount again. They feel relieved they've tried, it's a weight off their shoulders, but they won't push for it.

After that course, when people asked me for a discount, I'd say something like, *I'll tell you what, David, just let me have a look at the figures. Were you interested in a white one or a blue one? The blue one? Okay, let me just see if I've got one in stock.* Then I'd come back and say, *Yes, I've got one in stock*, or *No, I haven't but I can get one for Tuesday. I'll tell you what, Dave, if I can get you that blue one ready for Tuesday have we got a deal?*

And sure enough, the customers would never mention discount again. I learnt a huge lesson there and passed it on when teaching people to haggle in the show. I'd say, *Don't get sidetracked. If you ask the salesperson a question, make sure you get an answer*. There were lots of tips like that.

When I was a salesperson I always used humour. Some of my customers were quite switched on when it came to asking for money off. I had my own way of dealing with the situation and it went something like this:

CUSTOMER: Can I have a discount?

DOM: I'll tell you what, if you can spell discount I'm going to give it to you.

CUSTOMER: D-i-s-c-o-u-n-t.

DOM: No, you missed the F out. Spell it again.

CUSTOMER: There's no F in discount.

DOM: No effing discount. That's right. Now how do you want to pay?

CUSTOMER (laughing): I don't believe you – you're such a cheeky little . . . !

DOM: Exactly right. Come on, give us your money!

I had managed to steer the question about discount away and got on with the sale. It made them laugh and I always found humour helped things along. It's never good to be confrontational, whether you're buying or selling. Make haggling fun, remember it's a game. I really enjoy educating the public about the fact that you can get deals out there, because usually people just don't ask. I love the fact that when people watch the programme they feel empowered to go out and try it. I believe you can haggle for anything you buy.

Everything is possible.

Valuable lessons

When you get a great deal it's a buzz. I love it and I try to instil it into people. I don't just do it on TV, I do it with friends and family as well. My sister went through quite a bitter divorce. Her two kids were in their early teens and I said to them, *Look after your mum, you know, she's on her own, struggling a bit with money, you've got to be nice to her, don't give her a hard time*. They're great kids and they really supported her well, so when things were finally sorted out, I said, *Right, I'm going to reward you both. We're going to Lakeside Shopping Centre*. They were over the moon.

I knew they'd enjoy the day, but I wanted them to learn something from it too. So I said to them, *When we get there you can choose whatever you want. I'm not going to question what you buy, it's entirely up to you and I'll pay for it, up to two hundred pounds. If you get a discount on the item, then you've saved yourself some money and you've got more to spend. If you don't and you give up and I then get some discount, whatever I save is mine*. And they agreed to that.

My niece saw a Bench tracksuit she wanted to buy. It was priced up at £80. Like most people she was saying, *I won't get a discount*, but she knew she was duty-bound by me just to try it. The young girl she spoke to in the shop was probably about the same age as her, about fifteen or sixteen. My niece said, *Can I have a discount?* The Saturday girl said no. My niece came and told me she couldn't get a discount. She gave up at that point, so I went over to the girl on the till and politely asked who was in charge. She pointed out the manager, whose name was Dave.

I went up to him and said, *Dave, I'm treating my niece here to a tracksuit. It's £80, that's a lot of money. I like the tracksuit, not too keen on the price.* I didn't even need to ask for a discount. He asked if my niece was a college student and I said no. I never lie. I wouldn't, because to me that's deception, that's not getting a good deal. I just joked, *She's not now, might be one day!* Cheeky reply. He smiled and said, *That'll do,* then he called across to the girl on the till, *Give the student discount.* We got the tracksuit for £64, which was 20 per cent off, a saving of £16. My niece, and I admire her for doing this, said, *I've got sixteen more pounds!* I said, *Uh-uh, I've got sixteen more pounds.*

We carried on shopping like that and my niece was asking questions and wanted to learn. I was giving her the same advice I give people on *Don't Get Done, Get Dom.* Why didn't she get a discount on her tracksuit? She went to the wrong person. You have to use your common sense. She was asking someone the same age as her, who was obviously not even a full-time member of staff. There was no way a Saturday girl would have the authority to give a discount. You've got to speak to the right person. If you don't know who that is, ask and find out. Then get on first-name terms with them and talk about the product. Make it clear you're happy to buy it today . . . if the price is right though.

My nephew picked up on how to haggle very well. He was asking for discounts and being very cheeky. Shopkeepers quite like that old-fashioned bartering. It can be enjoyable, a nice experience, and he saved himself a little fortune. In the end he got about two hundred and forty pounds worth of spending . . . just because he asked for it. That's such a valuable lesson I've taught them both. It's the same when we're filming the series. When I help people who are nervous about haggling to get a deal on their big buy, it's a good feeling.

Viewers at home have learnt how to haggle too. I have been inundated with letters and emails from people saying how much the show has helped them. I had one recently from an elderly man who wrote to tell me he'd bought a car using the tips I give on TV.

He said, *I've wasted seventy-four years of my life! Until I saw your programme I would never have dreamed of bartering, but I've just got a discount on a car. I thoroughly enjoyed it and so did the salesperson. I'm writing with my sincere thanks for educating me on that. I wish I'd done it earlier.*

I really, really enjoy hearing from people like that.

A well-known face

I never get tired of haggling, I always enjoy the challenge, but being on TV means my face is better known these days and I often get a discount before I've even asked for it. The shopkeepers recognise me and say, *Okay Dom, I'll do you a deal!* I had that recently when I was out with a friend of mine who is a sergeant in the Territorial Support Group police force. He wanted to buy an iPod wall charger and it was priced up in the shop at £18. When the salesman went to the till he rang it up at £13.

My friend, who is as straight as a die, said *It's eighteen, isn't it?* The salesperson explained he'd given a staff discount.

When my mate asked why, the salesperson looked at me and said, *Because you're with him and I know he's going to ask for it in a minute!* We hadn't mentioned a discount, he just gave it to us. It really made me laugh and when we came out I said to my friend, *The lattes are on you!*

There are other times when people ask me to haggle when I really don't feel like it. I've been diabetic for 33 years. I don't have too much of a problem with it. I've never let it become a hurdle. But one day I was filming on Leigh-on-Sea beach and my sugar levels were low – it's a common thing, not a major problem. So I took a quick break and went to a local shop to buy a Twix. I think it was 45p, so I gave the lady 50p and instead of giving me my change she just looked at me. I asked what was wrong and she said, *You say you haggle on everything, so haggle!*

I'm thinking, Oh no, I really need to be eating this chocolate right now. I had to weigh up whether it would be easier to explain I'm diabetic, or just do a quick haggle. So I said 30p, she said 40p and I said done. If she'd only known, she could have got a fiver out of me for it. As I wolfed it down on the spot, I started to sweat and she was looking at me, thinking what's wrong with him? In the end I told her about my diabetes and she said, *I feel ever so bad now.*

But I saw the funny side.

Independent traders

People sometimes ask why we tend to favour independent traders over the big chains in the series and there is a reason for this. We don't warn anybody that we're filming, because that would be pointless. Deals don't happen that way, so we film secretly. As soon as we finish, we tell the retailer what we've done and ask them to sign a release form to allow us to use the footage.

Independent traders are usually very good about that. But the big chains have never, ever given us permission to use haggles filmed in their stores because they don't want anyone to see this. They are wary because they think they'd get everybody coming in doing exactly the same thing. They don't want it, so they never give us permission. That's why we have to avoid the big chains. That doesn't mean, however, that you can't get a discount in a chain store, because you can.

When I'm out shopping on my own, I haggle in big department stores all the time. I get discounts, no problem at all. In fact it's quite often easier than in independents. You see, a lot of big department stores have concessions inside them and those outlets have sales targets to hit from head office. They're desperate to do deals. I've been able to get discounts in every department store I've ever been into, even if you don't see it in the TV series.

Consumer champion

We're now working on *Don't Get Done, Get Dom* series four, which will be screened on BBC One in 2010. A lot of time and care goes into every programme. A team of people help me with all the background work that needs to be done, which is not part of the filming process. Lots and lots of research is needed for what we do. Making ten new programmes is a big commitment from everyone involved.

I absolutely thrive on the hard work. I don't work for money; I've been quite comfortable for a while. That's not the driving force for me . . . work is. It's a bit of an addiction really as I've always put work before settling down or having children or anything else. Last year I was doing between 100 and 110 hours some weeks, including travelling. I'm beginning to slowly swing around to the normal way of thinking now, and starting to think I should slow down a little bit. But no one ever died of hard work. You can die of stress, but not hard work. That's what I was brought up believing.

I am passionate about what I do. Hence the reason I'm quite good at not only getting deals and making shopping a bit more enjoyable, but also sorting out people's problems. The public have adopted me as their sort of 'voice of the people' – the consumer champion. I'm not egotistical, I don't want to big myself up, but if that's how they see me, I'm pleased. More than anything, I want to empower people and tell them they have every right to stand up for themselves in disputes and get the best deal they possibly can when spending their money.

In this book I'll show you how to be a winner in the credit crunch. Getting a great deal is enjoyable. I'll haggle over a packet of biscuits if I think I can get a discount. When you've read *Don't Get Done, Get Dom* I hope you'll feel the same way too.

Let's get started . . .

PART I

•

How To Haggle Like Dom

CHAPTER ONE

•

Do Your Research

'When you go out to buy the bargain of a lifetime, ignorance is not bliss!'

- **Start by setting your budget**
- **Research the product you want to buy**
- **Research extras – have some ready**
- **Get Out of Jail Card – a must-have**
- **Trial run – learn from your mistakes**
- **Confidence boost – respect yourself**
- **Mindset – stay cool**

START BY SETTING YOUR BUDGET

If *you* want to haggle like Dom and land that special bargain, you must focus every step of the way. Start by asking yourself an important question: *How much do I want to spend?*

Once you have set your budget, your target is to land a deal that offers the best possible value for that amount of money. As many people have discovered from his TV series, Dom can show you how to do that.

'Brits spend millions shopping, but we are renowned for being reserved and rarely ask for discounts,' says Dom. 'I want to change that.'

Most of the people he helps on *Don't Get Done, Get Dom* start out as very timid hagglers. In one show, Dom meets Joe who he describes as a shy family guy. Joe's wife says Joe is a great husband and father, but probably not the best person to haggle. Joe admits that bartering for a bargain 'will be a test'. With Dom's help, Joe builds his self-confidence and gets £500 off a £3,958 boiler, a saving of over 12 per cent. Joe also gets £550 worth of extras thrown in for free and this was with a major energy supplier, not an independent. It just shows what can be achieved when you 'Haggle Like Dom'!

Hard-up students can be equally embarrassed when it comes to bartering for a really good price. Matt is a young ice hockey player from Norwich. His skates cost £400, but he did not ask for a discount when he bought them. 'I feel shy around people I don't know well,' he admits. When Matt needs some new equipment, Dom steps in to help. Matt follows Dom's advice to the letter . . . and gets gear worth £630 for just £300. That's over 47 per cent off!

You will be surprised how far your budget can stretch, when you learn to haggle like Dom.

Research the product you want to buy

Whether you are buying a hot tub or a laptop, all products have their own special design features. But what do you really need from the product? There is no point in paying for extra features you will never use. Dom recommends doing your research, before you start spending money.

'Have a look round and find the product you think will best suit your needs and budget. Find out how much you can buy it for from other sources, including the internet. Give the shop you want to buy from a chance to compete with their rivals.'

Let's look at a couple of case studies from the series to see how this 'research' works.

Naz wants to buy a hot tub for his partner Tina. She has had leukaemia and the treatment has left her with soft-tissue damage in her back. Naz and the kids are sure a hot tub is just what Tina needs to help her relax at the end of the day.

It's a lovely idea, but there is a problem. Naz says he is 'totally useless' at haggling. He wants to get the price of the hot tub down, but admits he has not got the skills to do so. Dom is determined to help and takes Naz to a hot tub showroom to do some research. It's a good idea to plan your questions before you start your research. What do you want to know? If the sales staff are professional, they should be happy to share their knowledge, even when you make it clear you are not going to buy right away.

Naz discovers that delivery and fitting should be included

in the retail price. He is also told to ask for a free site survey to make sure the new hot tub will fit in his garden. The same applies to beds and furniture. Make sure they will go through the door, up the stairs, into the room, etc. Check the measurements before you buy and save yourself a lot of hassle.

(That advice may seem pretty obvious, but disasters do happen. One family on the South Coast ordered a hot tub only to find there was no easy way of getting it into their back garden. It was just too big. They had to hire a huge crane to lift the spa over their house and into the backyard. A very expensive mistake!)

Naz's research trip is a success. He leaves the showroom knowing the type of hot tub he needs to ease Tina's back pain. He knows what he wants to buy and why. He also realises he needs to shop at the top end of his budget of £13,000.

Single mum Samantha is another of Dom's nervous protégées. She tells him she would never dream of asking for a price cut or free extras. In fact, she is so nervous when out shopping she doesn't even like trying new clothes on for size. 'I just like to be in and out,' she says. That may sound extreme but if we're honest, many of us know that feeling.

Samantha wants to buy a laptop for her son Jack, who is dyslexic. She has saved £1,000 to buy the computer, but her research trip shows she does not need to spend that much. Laptops start from £399 and models priced from £499 to £599 should suit most requirements. The computer's hard drive is measured in gigabytes. The higher the gigabytes, the bigger the storage. Samantha learns that 40–60 gigabytes will be ideal for Jack's laptop. Like Naz, Samantha's research trip is very successful. She finds her £1,000 will easily pay for Jack's new laptop . . . plus some exciting extras.

Having done their research, Samantha and Naz go on to

get great deals when they haggle for real on *Don't Get Done, Get Dom*. They both walk away as winners . . .

Research extras – have some ready

Dom's advice is to always go for some extras as part of any deal you do. Before you start talking to the sales staff, have a look around the shop or showroom for extras you would like to get for free as part of your deal. Make your wish list realistic. You're not likely to persuade the salesperson to throw in expensive items as extras. But they may well include some free accessories to go with the product you are buying, if you tell them it will seal the deal.

Bonus!

The time to raise the subject is when you have haggled hard and you feel sure the salesperson won't drop any more on price. Know which extras to go for when the time comes for that final push.

Get Out of Jail Card – a must-have

When you've done your research, it's time for a trial run to see how good (or bad) you are at haggling. It's natural to feel nervous, but never let a smooth-talking salesperson push you into a purchase you're not sure you want to make. Dom has some great advice on how you can bail out if the going gets too tough.

'One thing you must have when you go into any selling environment is a Get Out of Jail Card,' Dom explains. 'By that I mean an excuse to get out of the shop if you find the pressure is getting a bit too intense. Have a reason ready . . . whatever you feel comfortable with. Give it a bit of thought, though. It has to be something the salesperson can't get round.

'If a customer says they want to talk things over with their wife/husband/partner before making a final decision, an experienced salesperson will say, *Let's call them now*. If a student says they need to see their parents about the money, the salesperson might say, *Let's drive round now, show them the car and if they like it we'll do a deal*. Good salespeople will overcome all those objections, because they're used to them.

'You've got to find reasons they can't argue with. For example:

- I've got a dentist's appointment in ten minutes. I can't cancel it. I've been waiting six weeks for this one.
- I've got to pick the kids up from school.
- My husband/wife/partner is ill. I can't talk to them about this until they're better.

'Those are some examples of good excuses to use if things start to feel a bit awkward in a shop and you want to get away. Pull that card out, use it and watch their faces drop because they know there's nothing they can say to stop you.'

Get Out of Jail Cards give you the chance to think things through in your own space and time.

Trial run – learn from your mistakes

If you have done your research, why do you need a trial run?

Well, once you are face-to-face with an experienced salesperson, you may find everything you've learnt goes clean out of your head. Naz found that with his hot tub trial run. Samantha was the same with her laptop practice session. On

Don't Get Done, Get Dom, Dominic listens on headphones as his protégés test their haggling skills, then talks to them about what they can learn from the experience.

Obviously, Dom won't be with you when you do your trial run, so why not take someone you trust? Ask them to say nothing at all. They are there to listen. Afterwards they can give you their honest advice on how you dealt with the salesperson. What was good and what was bad? It's a great way to learn. And remember the Golden Rule. *Never* buy anything on a trial run unless you have had such a successful haggle it's worth doing. If you're in danger of doing that, use your Get Out of Jail Card to get away from the salesperson in a hurry!

Confidence boost – respect yourself

There are three things you need to 'Haggle Like Dom': confidence, confidence and more confidence!

Doing your research and a trial run will certainly help. So will the security of knowing you can use your Get Out of Jail Card if the going gets tough. But why not give yourself an extra boost? Dom does just that with Naz who is afraid of heights. Dom asks him to climb an abseiling wall and climb down again. Obviously, all safety aspects are provided, but the wall is still a major test. When Naz gets back down to the ground again he is all smiles and walks away feeling really good about himself.

Naz was lucky to have Dom to encourage him, but why not think about your own confidence booster? Look for a challenge you would like to safely overcome and which will get you used to being outside your comfort zone for a while. When you've passed that test, haggling for a good deal won't seem so daunting. You'll be in the mood to come away with a great result. Every time you get a good deal after that, your self-belief will grow higher and higher. With your confidence running high, the only way is up!

Mindset – stay cool

Now you're ready to go for the real deal!

So, does that mean you should psyche yourself up to argue and scrap for a brilliant buy? No, that's not the way. Dom's advice is much more subtle than that. He describes it this way:

'When I go in to buy something, I look at the price and I think, Let's have a bit of a game. Let's just see if I can get some money off. Nobody's going to get hurt. Nobody's going to get embarrassed. If you don't get it [a big reduction], you don't get it . . .'

In other words, what have you got to lose?

Dom always stays ice cool when he is haggling. There is no need to be rude. A cheeky smile and a bit of humour are much more effective. If a salesperson likes you and thinks you're being reasonable, they are much more likely to do a deal. But you do need to be confident. Go into a store looking naïve and lost and sales staff can be like a pack of hyenas. They will tear you apart if you are not careful.

But do your research before you go for the real deal and you'll be all set to win the salesperson's respect. They will see they've met their match. The best deals are sealed with a handshake . . . and smiles all round. So, stay cool, stay focused and make it fun. That's the perfect mindset.

Okay, time to go shopping . . .

Dom says: Make haggling fun. Remember, it's just a game!

CHAPTER TWO

•

Make A Winning Start

'If you've got a nice smile, you're halfway there.'

- **Walk in with energy and enthusiasm**
- **Get the salesperson's name**
- **Be friendly – build a good relationship**
- **Know about the product**
- **Have fun but stay focused**

WALK IN WITH ENERGY AND ENTHUSIASM

I'm here to haggle . . . and I feel good!

That's the perfect mindset as you walk into your chosen shop, showroom or store on the day of your big buy. Leave any doubts, worries and negative thoughts far behind. You've got all Dom's haggling tips in mind and you're ready to go.

Dom meets a complete cross-section of shoppers in *Don't Get Done, Get Dom* and many of them get their relationship with the sales staff off to the wrong start. Some look nervous, some look grumpy, and some look aggressive and ready for an argument. The truth is they are all feeling a bit nervous about haggling and they cover it in different ways.

What's the answer? Simple, really: don't build the sales staff into monsters.

Welsh student Natalie was nervous about haggling before meeting Dom.

'What's the big problem?' Dom asks her.

'Being told to get out of the shop for being so cheeky,' says Natalie.

'Have you ever had that?' Dom asks.

'No,' Natalie admits.

'There's no reason to fear it, if it's never happened,' Dom tells her. 'It's never likely to happen. You're spending money! You can always be cheeky as long as you're nice, that's the main thing.'

Natalie has conjured up pictures of an embarrassing scenario in her mind. But no shop is going to throw you out for asking for a better price. Obviously, if a customer is rude or arrogant, sales staff may get upset or annoyed. That's human nature. But if you are pleasant and polite, like Natalie, you should have no problems at all.

In fact, after some coaching from Dom, Natalie goes on to make a terrific saving when she buys a £1,799 telescope she needs for her studies for just £1,549. That's a star discount of £250, achieved with no embarrassment whatsoever.

Yes, haggling can be great fun, especially when it goes well, but you must be on your toes right from the start. You need to *accentuate the positive* and *eliminate the negative* when you're out for a big buy.

From the moment you walk into the shop you must say and do the right things.

Your first haggle is sure to be the toughest. So, why not practise the right way of doing things at home? It might seem a bit offbeat, but it works. Don't be embarrassed. Famous actors practise their lines at home all the time. Some of the best scenes you have ever seen on TV or at the movies have been perfected off-screen. Practice makes perfect!

When you set out to haggle, you are playing a part. There's no doubt about that. So get your lines right for the big performance. Forget your inhibitions and just go for it. Try talking to the mirror at home. Imagine you're talking to the salesperson. How do you look? Edgy and nervous, or bright and keen to do a deal? Get used to avoiding negative phrases like 'I don't suppose . . .', 'you wouldn't be able to . . .' and 'you couldn't give . . .'. Keep smiling and stay positive. As Dom says, practise, practise, practise. Get comfortable with his haggling tips and use them well.

Don't waste time dreaming up all the things that could go wrong when you start haggling. Focus on how good you will feel when you play the game for real and win. Sales staff deal with timewasters every day of the week. People who walk in with absolutely no intention of spending their money, but you're not like that. You mean business, if the price is right.

You are the customer every salesperson is waiting for!

Get the salesperson's name

What is the first thing you should do when you meet the salesperson? Smile and ask their first name. Then use it as often as you can in the conversation. Give them your name too. It's amazing how a simple gesture like that can start to break down barriers. You're not dealing with a monster. Just someone like you, but doing their job.

The best haggles happen when there is goodwill on both sides.

Being on first-name terms is an excellent start.

'I studied some research that was done in America,' says Dom. 'It was all about the psychology of selling and it was so true. It showed that a simple gesture like shaking hands really can break down invisible barriers. I do that when I'm shopping. Shake hands with the salesperson and ask their name right away.'

It works for Dom and it will work for you too.

Be friendly – build a good relationship

Building a good relationship with the salesperson is vital. Try seeing things from their point of view. Working in a shop or showroom can mean long hours and a fair amount of tedium. So, when a customer walks in who is friendly and keen to buy, it can come as a very pleasant change.

Don't get tongue-tied. Some light-hearted chat before you

start talking business is always a good start. If you're stuck for an idea, just talk about the weather. It really doesn't matter what you talk about, as long as you start to break the ice.

Top Tip: Don't start haggling or talk about price for the first five minutes you're with a salesperson

At the back of your mind you know you want to drive the hardest bargain you can, but that does not mean you can't have some fun along the way. Humour plays a big part in the way Dom approaches any haggle. He always has a joke with the sales staff.

'All our products are guaranteed,' says a salesperson in *Don't Get Done, Get Dom.*

Dom's not buying that line.

'*Everything's* guaranteed these days!' he smiles.

The salesperson laughs. He knows his sales line has been twigged. Nice try though!

Laughter and a bit of banter are always welcome at the start of a haggle.

Be friendly!

Know about the product

This is where your research comes into play. By following Dom's guidelines, you will have looked around and will know what you want to buy and why. You will also know the official retail price for that item and which outlets, including the internet, are offering the best deals on it.

Why is this important?

Once again, put yourself in the salesperson's shoes. Let's look at two imaginary scenes:

1. A customer comes in looking a bit timid and says they are looking for a washing machine. They don't know which make or style they want to see and they have no clear idea of the features they need or how much they want to spend.
2. Another customer comes in and greets you with a smile. They are also looking for a washing machine, but this time they know the model and brand they're interested in. You say there are some other good machines on the market at the moment and they're happy to hear more. Then they ask your opinion on the relative merits of front and top loaders and what you think of the new steam feature many washing machines are now offering. It's clear they respect your knowledge and want to hear what you have to say.

Which of these people would you respect most?

We can't blame salespeople for making the most of customers who wander in like lost sheep. If you go into a big buy totally unprepared you are asking for trouble. To be honest, the salesperson will see you coming. Their job is to make the best sale they can and a nervy, naïve punter will give them every chance of doing just that. So, make sure you're not that naïve punter. Have some basic knowledge of what you want to buy before you go shopping.

In one episode of *Don't Get Done, Get Dom,* Marlon wants to buy an engagement ring for Julie. When he first meets Dom, he admits he knows nothing about rings and even less about haggling. Marlon's budget is £2,000 and unless he learns some lessons quickly, he could easily spend the lot.

'When I go into a shop and see a price tag, that to me is the price,' Marlon explains. 'It wouldn't occur to me that I could get it for anything other than that.'

Marlon feels asking for a discount could cause confrontation, but Dom assures him that is not the case.

'It's all good fun as long you don't offend or annoy them [the sales staff] and wind them up.'

With that positive message ringing in his ears, Marlon does some instant research into rings within his budget. In no time he knows he is looking for 0.5 karat diamond set in an 18 karat white gold ring. Sounds lovely. Now to get the price down!

Marlon goes into a jeweller's and instantly creates a good impression by knowing what he wants to buy. He stays polite and focused through the negotiations and, with Dom's help, Marlon buys a £1,950 engagement ring for just £1,350. That's a superb saving of £600! He evens gets 12 red roses, a box of chocolates and a bottle of champagne thrown in for free, as extras in the deal. In return he promises the shop owner he will bring Julie in to look for her wedding ring. By doing a good deal, the jeweller will benefit from future business.

The shop owner wishes Marlon well. 'I think he was a very nervous person, but he took quite a courageous step and in the end he has obviously got fantastic value, he really has.'

No hard feelings. No confrontation. Just the warm glow that comes from a deal well done. If you want to feel that way after your big buy, make sure you make the right start. And having a good conversation with the salesperson about the product you plan to buy is definitely the way to go.

Have fun but stay focused

Obviously, Dom is a natural when it comes to haggling. He admits he will barter for *anything*. He loves it and we can all learn money-saving tips from him. One thing is certain. Dom may joke and laugh with sales staff, but his mind is always completely focused during a haggle. You must follow his lead in your big buy.

Have fun . . . but remember why you are there.

Like Marlon buying that special diamond ring, you want the bargain of a lifetime!

Dom says: It's easier to be nice to someone than to be aggressive or hard. It burns up more energy. Why would you want to do that in life?

CHAPTER THREE

Don't Haggle Too Soon

'I'm just the right person to give a few lessons on haggling.'

- **Don't rush to do the deal**
- **Let the salesperson talk about the product**
- **Keep an open mind**
- **Make it clear you can buy today**
- **Make your move – when the time is right**

DON'T RUSH TO DO THE DEAL

In *Don't Get Done, Get Dom* the advice to viewers is *don't haggle too soon*. If you are going for a big buy, something you have been saving up for, don't rush to do the deal.

Take your time and think carefully about what you are doing, every step of the way. Patience is a virtue. That message comes through loud and clear.

In one show, Dom meets an 18-year-old student called Chris who is a very talented footballer. His career has been disrupted by injuries and he needs a home gym to build up his fitness. Dom meets Chris at St James' Park, home of his soccer heroes Newcastle United. Chris does a trial run in a local sports shop to see how he gets on with haggling.

Chris gets off to a good start. He is soon on first-name terms with the salesperson and tells him about the injuries he has had. He asks for advice on what kind of gym equipment will give him the help he needs. Everything is going well until Chris asks how much discount the salesperson will give him . . . *before he even knows what the gym costs*.

That is not the way to go!

Chris has a laugh with Dom about it later and learns an important lesson. When it comes to haggling, don't rush in like a bull in a china shop. With Dom's help, Chris learns to stay in control and goes on to haggle £270 off an £870 new home gym, a saving of over 31 per cent.

Chris's main problem was youthful enthusiasm and most sales staff will deal with that quite happily. But when a customer is aggressive, that's another matter. Being too direct can cause tension and that's not good when you are looking for a bargain. Paul is a salesperson and another of Dom's guests on *Don't Get Done, Get Dom*. Paul admits he can be 'a bit over the top' when looking for good deals when he is out shopping. His wife Debbie says if she was selling to him she would not give him a discount because he is too 'abrupt'. 'He's a nightmare – he goes in for the kill all the time.'

Most of the people who come to Dom for help are nervous about haggling. Paul is the opposite. 'I haven't got the time to go all the way around the bushes to get to a deal,' he says, when he first appears on the show. 'I think most of what I buy is done in minutes. It's like, in . . . *am I going to get a deal? No I'm not. You keep it, I'll go next door.*'

'Paul's hard line in bartering means shopping trips can get heated,' Dom explains. 'Wife Debbie walks away and daughter Chloe thinks she can get a better discount than her dad, who often loses a great deal because of his stubbornness. I reckon Paul's a pussy cat underneath. He's just got to learn to show his softer side while he's negotiating. It's simple really, if a salesperson likes you and thinks you're being reasonable, they are much more likely to do a deal.'

Paul admits he often walks out of shops 'out of sheer temper' if the salesperson does not give him the price he wants. Now Dom wants to show him how to get a top deal on a new caravan, without rubbing anyone up the wrong way. First he needs to see Paul in haggling action. They go to a local caravan dealership for a trial run. Paul is fired up and ready to go. 'I'm feeling wonderful. I'm just ready to get in there and get the right deal.'

'Getting a deal's one thing,' says Dom with a smile. 'Don't go in there for a fight.'

Dom tells the viewers: 'Through this practice run I will be able to see just how pushy our Paul really is. He is no stranger to getting a discount, but the way he goes about it is quite often not the best approach. He *expects* a discount and that quite often puts salespeople's backs up. I want to see him pace himself before even asking for one.'

Dom is never aggressive when looking for a good buy. He knows getting on well with the sales staff is all-important. 'Never undermine a salesperson,' he says. 'Allow them to do their job, knowing that at the end of the day their job is to get a good deal accompanied by a smile.'

On his trial run, Paul breaks just about all of Dom's top tips on successful haggling.

1. He does not ask the salesperson's name.
2. He does not chat or joke with the salesperson to build rapport.
3. He haggles too soon.
4. He undermines the salesperson by laughing at the price he quotes.

'He's like Speedy Gonzales,' says Dom, who is listening in from a nearby car. 'Right away he's asked for discount. He's been there less than two minutes. What he should have done here is build up a bit of banter. I think it would have helped the whole situation.'

Paul does get the offer of £495 discount on a £9,995 caravan, but did he get the bottom line? Dom does not think so. The salesperson confirms that he thought Paul's approach was too direct. 'He seemed to go for the jugular too quickly in the negotiations.'

Not a great result, but Paul is happy to move on and take Dom's advice on board. He gets some tips on tact and leaves what Dom calls his 'all guns blazing approach' behind. When it comes to doing the real deal, Paul goes into a caravan showroom with clear guidelines from Dom . . .

1. Don't mention discount during the first five minutes with the salesperson.
2. Don't haggle on the price at all during that time.
3. Allow the salesperson to settle into the conversation as well as you.

Paul's whole approach is different on this occasion. He builds a rapport with the salesperson and soon finds a suitable caravan priced at £18,380. Negotiations stall and rather than get aggravated Paul walks away peacefully, but only to gather his thoughts and have a quick word with Dom.

Top Tip: Use whatever bargaining chips you have

Paul goes back and offers his own caravan in part exchange for the new one. Paul has already had an offer elsewhere of £11,000 for his caravan. After a little haggling, he and the salesperson agree on a part-exchange payment of £4,800 for the new caravan originally priced at £18,380. By being patient Paul has saved the equivalent of over £2,500 (over 14 per cent), and he is delighted.

'I have to admit, normally I would have gone in there and said, *How much is that?* Bang, bang and gone for a low price. But Dom told me to hold back and ask some more questions and slow the pace down. It worked. I got on well with the salesperson and he gave me a discount!'

The salesperson feels good about the deal too. 'He's happy and we're happy.'

It just goes to show that patience isn't just a virtue, *it's a money saver too!*

Rushing in to haggle too soon is a mistake, but so is not haggling at all.

That's what teacher Emma learns when she does a trial

run in *Don't Get Done, Get Dom*. Emma worked in Mexico for three years and met her husband there. Bartering is a way of life in that part of the world, but Emma admits she is still 'pretty terrible' at haggling. Now she wants to buy a new family bathroom and Dom is keen to help, but first he needs to find out more about her negotiating skills.

Dom asks Emma to get the best deal she can on one of the items in a bathroom showroom. He listens in to the conversation, so he can pinpoint where she goes wrong. Emma tells the salesperson she is looking for a new shower. He shows her a top-of-the-range remote control model. It costs £2,200, which is way above Emma's budget, but this is her chance to practise getting the price down.

Emma can't hear Dom, but he can hear her from a nearby car and is willing her on.

'Come on, Emma, just ask for some money off. See what happens.'

Emma tells the salesperson she is just looking around and won't be buying anything today. This is not a good start. Why would the salesperson give you much attention if there was no sale to be had? Emma should have said 'I wasn't planning on buying today but if the price was right I could be tempted.'

'She's not going to ask for discount here,' says Dom. 'She's so worried about the salesperson saying no, she's not even going to bother asking. The main reason she didn't get a price drop was because she didn't even ask for one.'

When she meets Dom outside the store, he asks why she didn't ask for a discount.

'Scared he would say no,' Emma admits.

'If you don't try, you won't succeed,' says Dom.

Emma knows Dom is right. She follows his advice and goes on to get a great deal on a new bathroom suite. But the way Emma felt at first is not unusual. Many of us are ill at ease when it comes to trying to get a good deal. That's why it makes such good sense not to rush. Let your big buy develop at a gentle pace. Don't walk away from the salesperson, get to know them better. There is no need to feel edgy about haggling – you're not at that stage yet.

So relax and use the following ideas to help you bag a bargain.

Let the salesperson talk about the product

It's always good to let the salesperson tell you about the product you want to buy. You may know a bit already from the research you've done, but it relaxes them, and it's polite to listen to the information you are being given. It makes sense too.

'The salesperson should know more about the products they are selling than you do,' says Dom. 'So it's good to go in and give them a chance to recommend what's new. Let them show you the stock on offer. They may be able to offer a discount on a certain model because it hasn't got the latest features. If you don't need those new additions, you could do a deal on the old stock that will suit you and the salesperson.'

Lots of people go into a haggle seeing the salesperson as an enemy, but Dom always keeps an open mind. He is more than capable of dealing with a sharp salesperson. But he gives good salespeople the respect they deserve. That is part of the philosophy he applies when doing a deal on *Don't Get Done, Get Dom*.

'What people forget is that sales staff often feel quite nervous to start with, just like you,' Dom explains. 'You need to break down the barriers between you and conversation does that. You'll soon break the ice and start enjoying yourselves by having a bit of a laugh and a giggle. Allow the salesperson to share their wealth of knowledge about their products. Listen and learn. Quite often I've gone to buy something and the salesperson's said, *Do you realise that model is being superseded in a month's time?* And I say, *No I don't, what's coming out?* That's specialist knowledge and it's very helpful.'

Conversation also gives you the opportunity to find out a little more about the person you are dealing with. If their sales pitch is swift and slick and you feel they are trying to steamroller you into a deal simply because that product will earn them the most commission, make sure they don't get away with it. Stand your ground and keep asking questions. See how much the salesperson really knows about what they're trying to sell you. Make sure you, not they, are in control of the situation. That's important: being rushed into parting with your money is bad news. Buy in haste, repent at leisure. Remember that Get Out of Jail Card.

If the salesperson only seems interested in grabbing your cash as soon as possible, you have the right to walk away. When Dom is talking to his protégés on the show, he tells them to have that Get Out of Jail Card ready. A simple excuse to leave the store and try elsewhere.

Dom knows all the tricks salespeople use inside out, but if you get good service in a shop, store or showroom, his advice is to let the staff know you are impressed.

'Good salespeople know what they're talking about, really know their onions. They like the fact they have a wealth of knowledge and take pride in telling you exactly what you want to know. It gives them a good feeling. Great! That's the way it should be.'

By treating salespeople with respect, you build up a good

relationship and that will certainly help to smooth the way forward when negotiations start.

It's nice to be nice . . . and a little flattery goes a long way!

Keep an open mind

Careful research will have given you a clear idea of the product you wish to buy, but it pays to stay flexible on that choice. Let sales staff know if you have an open mind on colour, materials, etc. They may be able to offer you a better deal on the stock they have available. Of course, if you know *exactly* what you want, make sure you get it.

A salesperson may try to push you into buying an alternative product. If that happens, be sure to ask some leading questions. How does it differ from your chosen model? How does it rate on quality, efficiency and reliability? If the new product is inferior, the salesperson may try to change the subject, so don't get sidetracked.

You want straight answers to straight questions, or you're not buying.

If, on the other hand, the salesperson is pleasant and professional, it makes sense to hear what they have to say about similar products. Are they cheaper? If so, why? Does the alternative model have all the features you need and want? Can a lesser-known brand really match up to its famous competitor when it comes to quality? Are you just paying more for the brand name?

Those are some of the questions you might like to ask. Stay flexible and keep an open mind, but do be wary. Listen to everything that is said, then weigh it all up carefully in your own mind. Take your time. Make sure *you* make the final decision when the time comes . . . whatever the salesperson says!

Make it clear you can buy today

Dom always encourages people to be positive with sales staff from the start.

'If the price is right, I'm going to buy this today.'

That is a good, clear statement of intent. The salesperson knows right away they are in with a chance of selling you something and that's what they are there for.

Another of Dom's top tips is to let the shop know you are happy to pay any way they choose. Cash is nearly always best because the shop then avoids paying fees to your credit card company. These fees can vary, but they can cost shops thousands of pounds a year. Of course, the salesperson will always prefer to make a credit card sale than no sale at all, but cash is always welcome. Ask the salesperson what method will get you the best price.

Although you are not yet ready to haggle, it's good to drop these positive messages into your conversation with the salesperson at this stage. You can bet your bottom dollar they will be instantly noted and will play a part in getting you the best possible price, when the time comes.

Make your move – when the time is right

Question: How do you know when it's time to haggle?

Answer: When you can tick everything on this checklist:

1. Are you on first-name terms with the salesperson?
2. Have you built up some rapport by chatting with them?
3. Have they told you everything you want to know

about the product you plan to buy?

4. Have you carefully considered other products you have been shown?
5. Are you sure you are ready to buy?

If your answer to all those questions is yes, it's time to talk numbers.

Dom says: Remember, never ever go in and negotiate straight away.

CHAPTER FOUR

Let's Talk Numbers

'It doesn't enter my mind not to ask for discount.'

- **Play it cool on price**
- **Make your first offer so low it's almost insulting**
- **Know when to stay silent**
- **Use all your bartering chips**
- **Keep pushing for the best price**

PLAY IT COOL ON PRICE

All of Dom's advice so far has been leading up to this moment. The start of the haggle. Let's talk numbers . . .

You must play it cool when the salesperson asks the inevitable question: *How much have you got to spend?* Dom's thoughts on this are crystal clear. Never let them know your maximum budget. If you do, a smart salesperson's eyes will light up and they will want you to spend the lot, even trying to push you over your limit. Giving that information away can hurt a haggle before it has even begun.

You don't want to spend your maximum budget. That's the whole point of bartering. So, play your cards close to your chest. From your research you should know the retail price of the item you want to buy. Even if the shop is charging less than that, don't look pleasantly surprised. In fact, Dom always tells his protégés to look shocked and disappointed when the salesperson mentions price for the first time . . . whatever it is!

'Look as if you've just sucked a lemon,' he says.

On *Don't Get Done, Get Dom* it's surprising how often prices tumble before the haggling has even started in earnest, especially when the customer has taken the time to build that all-important relationship with the salesperson. Minimum not maximum: that's the price you're aiming for when you start to talk numbers.

It's so important to stay positive at this stage, but many people sound negative without even realising it. That's a must to avoid, as Dom reminds his protégé Ian when they meet on *Don't Get Done, Get Dom.* Ian is recovering from a heart attack. Golf gives him the healthy exercise he needs and he wants to treat himself to a new set of clubs. But when he does a trial run to practise his haggling, he makes the mistake many of us would make.

He is not positive enough.

Let's look at some examples of what Ian says and what Dom would prefer to hear. Ian can't hear Dom's comments at this stage, but they tell the viewers all they need to know.

The golf shop salesperson says the set of clubs Ian likes costs £529.

IAN: I've sort of seen them on the internet for about 480-odd quid.

DOM: What are you saying Ian? *I've sort of seen them on the internet*. You *have* seen them. Tell the guy that and you want a much better price. 'Sort of' shows signs of nervousness.

IAN (to salesperson): Would you budge at all?

DOM: You need to say, *How much can you budge?*

IAN: If you could get it down to sort of around five hundred quid, I'll probably look to buy them fairly soon.

DOM: You need to say, *I'll tell you what, if you can get that down well below £500 I'm buying today!*

Ian is not used to haggling. When he meets Dom later, he does not realise how badly his trial run has gone. 'I don't think it could have gone any better than that,' he says.

Dom has to be cruel to be kind. 'I'm going to shoot you down in flames. It wasn't very good at all,' he tells Ian. Dom says he admired him for trying to get some discount – many people are too scared to do that – but the way he went about it was too negative.

Avoid using phrases like:

- *I don't suppose . . .*
- *There's no chance you could . . .*
- *Would you mind if . . .*
- *You don't do any lower than that . . .*

If you ask the salesperson tentative questions like that, the answer you will get is NO!

If you *don't suppose* the shop will give you a deal, why should they do it? You need to be more confident. Dom tells Ian to practise asking his questions in a positive way.

- Don't say – *I don't suppose you can knock any money off?*
- Do say – *I like those . . . get the price down and I'll buy them today.*
- Don't say – *I don't suppose you could give me a discount?*
- Do say – *What sort of deal can you do to persuade me to buy today?*

Now those are great statements of intent.

Know what to say and how to say it. Ian learns the lesson well and goes on to buy a new set of golf clubs and a driver, plus extras including golf balls, a brolly and driving range tokens. Total price should be £961, but Neil lands the lot for just £640. That's a 33 per cent plus saving of £321. 'The best deal of my life!' he says with a smile.

Ian saved money and you can too. Just play it cool.

Make your first offer so low it's almost insulting

If you are not used to bartering, making a very low first offer may feel embarrassing, but you must do it. Ask Dom.

'When I send people in to buy various products on the show, nobody knows what the markup is on that item, including me,' he explains. 'It's the same for everyone. How do you know if the salesperson's got a 300 per cent profit margin to play with? Is it 10 per cent or even lower? You really have no idea. No one knows the markup on every product out there on the street.

'To get a good deal there is only one thing you can do and that is to go in so low with your first offer you know the shop can't possibly sell to you at that price. It's no good offering £95 for something that costs £100. If the shop says yes, you'll never know how much you could have got it for. Go in so low it's almost insulting, but do it in a friendly way that invites the salesperson to come back to you. If they say, *You must be joking, it cost us more than that* . . . great! You've gone in at the right price, established the floor, and now you can move on from there.'

Salespeople don't mind a cheeky offer, as long as you stay pleasant and polite. They know haggling is a game. They are experienced in it and enjoy dealing with a good negotiator. Dom has a saying that sums the whole thing up.

'I kick them in the gutter, pull them out of the trees and meet them on the pavement.'

In other words, the salesperson starts high on price, you start low. Hopefully you then meet somewhere in between (on the pavement!) and the deal is done.

You may not really expect the salesperson to accept your first offer, but say it like you mean it then wait. At this point don't speak. Allow the salesperson to answer first. Remember, choose your words carefully.

- Don't sound apologetic
- Do sound confident

'What you need to say to them is, *I love this product, but I don't like the price. It's a bit more than I want to spend. Take fifty quid for it and I will buy it now?* Sound like you mean it when you go in with a low offer, but maybe have a little smile on your face. You know you're being cheeky, they know you're being cheeky, so have a giggle with them.

'If you go in low, they will come back with a much better price than they would have originally said. Ask for discount on a £100 item and they'll give you a fiver. Offer £50 for that same product and they may say, *I'll do it for eighty*, because they know you've set your sights so low a fiver off is not going to interest you.

'That's part of the psychology of selling . . .'

Know when to stay silent

When you make an offer in a haggle, don't speak again until the salesperson replies. 'Some people immediately say, *I can stretch to a bit more if you can't do it for that*. They weaken their attack straight away,' explains Dom. If you say too much you sound anxious, as if you are trying to justify the offer you've just made. Dom knows these key moments of silence, when the price is left hanging in the air, are crucial to doing a great deal.

'The next one to speak is the loser, believe me,' he says. 'Salespeople know that. It's a technique they use. They ask a question – *If I give you a hundred pound off have we got a deal?* – then they stay silent. That's the salesperson's game. I'm teaching people to turn the tables and use it back on them.'

Dom knows body language is very important too.

'When you make your offer, nod your head very slightly as you do it. Be positive. Say something like, *Okay, I'll give you two hundred, have we got a deal?* Then look them in the eyes and give that little nod. It's psychology. Their brain is reading a subliminal message that's saying yes, not no. It's all about sending out positive messages and if you switch on to those, it can work wonders.'

When you face a long silence during a haggle, it can play on your nerves. But stay calm and follow Dom's advice. Wait for the salesperson to speak first, however long that takes. It's up to them to respond and they will. Eventually.

Make sure all they get from you is the sound of silence . . .

Use all your bartering chips

Unless you are amazingly lucky or have gone in low enough, the next step in the game will be for the salesperson to say your offer is way too low! That's no problem. It gives you the chance to ask another key question. *What is your best price?* When they say my best price is £xxx, don't believe it. It's part of their game plan and can always be lower.

Now the haggling really starts. Never accept the salesperson's first offer. If they come back with a question, answer with one of your own.

'For example,' Dom explains, 'the retailer may say, *If I give you a hundred off, have we got a deal?* Avoid saying yes or no. It's better to say, *Make it a hundred and fifty and we've got a deal. Can you do it?* That's a good way to turn it round, because the person asking the questions is always the one in control. Just like Anne Robinson on *The Weakest Link*!

'Salespeople ask lots of questions, they're trained to do it. And that's what you need to do to empower yourself in shops. The salesperson might ask, *If I throw in some free DVDs, have we got a deal?* Ignore that question and come back with one of your own. *I'll tell you what, if you throw in some DVDs and free delivery and a tuner and that scart lead you said I'd need, I'll do a deal. Yes or no?* Throw the ball back into their court. It's all a game . . . the psychology of selling.'

You want the maximum discount and you will need to use all your bartering chips to get it. Let's look at some of Dom's top tips on how to get that price right down.

Let them know they've got rivals. Whether you are dealing with a salesperson in a showroom or a builder at your house, tell them you've got quotes and prices from rival companies. This will make them try harder to get your business there and then, rather than risk a competitor beating them to it. It will help in getting the best price. Make it clear you are organised and no pushover. Tell them the price you want, when the time is right but remember initially to keep it very low. If you've found a really good deal on a website, have a printout ready to show them. Say you would rather buy from them, but only if they can challenge that internet price.

In the competitive world we live in, all salespeople hate being beaten, especially by a local rival. Dom often uses this to his advantage in *Don't Get Done, Get Dom*. In one high street haggle, he meets Roger who is looking for a new lawnmower. Roger has done his research and knows that the model he wants retails at £300. Can Dom get it any cheaper? Roger gives him an hour to find out . . .

The first shop Dom visits already has the mower discounted to £270.

Top Tip: Never accept the salesperson's first price. Always barter, even on discounted items

Dom keeps pushing for a discount and gets the lawnmower down to £260 plus a free pint of oil and a fuel container. Not bad, but Dom is sure he can do better elsewhere. Also, he is now able to play one shop off against the other.

Dom walks into the second lawnmower shop looking confident and gets on first-name terms with salesperson Charles straight away. Dom tells him he has been offered a good deal with some extras by a rival shop, but does not reveal the saving. He asks Charles for his best price.

Top Tip: Don't give away the rival salesperson's offer too soon

The lawnmower is £285 in this shop, but because Charles knows he is up against a rival he checks on prices, then asks Dom how £268 sounds. Dom says it's better, but not as good as he got elsewhere. Dom now outlines the deal already on offer and says he'd like to break the £250 bracket if he can.

'So what did I just say?' asks Charles. '£268?'

'I think it was £248?' jokes Dom. 'I can't remember.'

Top Tip: Cheeky humour can help a deal

Charles laughs and says, 'Last price, £245. How's that?' He also matches the extras included in the deal by the rival shop.

Dom holds out his hand and says, '£240, you've got a deal.'

Charles and Dom shake hands. This proves the point that the salesperson's 'last price' is always negotiable a bit further.

Top Tip: Remember Dom's mantra – push, push, push

Roger is very happy with the £60 saving on his new lawnmower.

'Do you want to know what the secret is to getting a discount?' says Dom. 'Asking for it in the first place. If you aren't wearing socks, you can't pull them up!'

Another of Dom's favourite ploys is to ask the salespeople he meets a simple question.

Have you got plenty in stock?

If the answer is yes, he knows they will want to get that stock shifted. Useful information when you're looking for a bargain. On the other hand, if the shop does not have the item in stock, that may work for you too. You can save money when something is ordered especially for you. Politely tell the salesperson they are getting a guaranteed sale and profit margin on an item they haven't even brought in yet and you want some of that. You can say it in a jovial way, but mean it!

Playing your bartering chips can be fun, but sometimes you do need to be serious. Don't be embarrassed to say you can't afford the price the salesperson is asking. It's a simple and direct way of telling them where you stand. But be sure to make it clear that the money you *have* got available is ready to be spent today if the deal is right. That's music to the ears of retailers.

Any place, any time, anywhere!

'Most people are too embarrassed to haggle in a posh shop,' says Dom. 'But between you and me, all shops are the same. They all mark up their products, they all have overheads to pay and let's face it, most of them will give a discount if it means them getting the business instead of their competitors.'

The key to successful bargaining is to tell yourself all things are possible. Be 100 per cent positive and see where it leads you. Would you ever think of asking for extra money off in a sale? Well, Dom does just that in *Don't Get Done, Get Dom* and it works for him. He sees a set of sheets that have been reduced from £59.99 to £39.00. Dom asks the salesperson if she can drop the price a bit more. She says he can have them for £35. Dom offers £29.99 and keeps asking in a funny, jovial way. The light-hearted banter ends well for Dom. He gets the sheets for £29.99.

Of course, to get a great bargain you must be sure to deal with the person who can give a discount. It's important not to undermine the salesperson you have been talking to. Ask them who is the best person to give you a good price. If it is not them, find out who it is. Ask their name and request to speak to them directly. Using their name will help to break down barriers. Make the meeting positive. Say you will be buying today if the price is right. This should provide a good result all round. Doing deals the Dom way always comes back to staying polite, even when you are pushing hard.

When haggling to win, it pays to use all your bartering chips.

Keep pushing for the best price

The best deals come when you hang in there and barter with the salesperson until you are absolutely sure they have gone as low on price as they possibly can. The final stages of a haggle can be the toughest and that is when you need to stay calm and focused. Keep the pressure on, but don't get intense or tetchy. Maintain the goodwill you have built up along the way and stay in the game. Your first goal is to get something off, no matter how little to start with.

'Be ready for objections from salespeople,' says Dom. 'When you first ask for a discount most of them will automatically say no. It's natural, that's what they learn on page one of the salesperson's bible. *Don't give discounts*. Having said that, some might knock something off right away, but you'll need to ask others five times or more. Normally, it will take three objections before you start to win the battle. The main priority here is to get any discount you can, even a pound, because once that happens the floodgates open. The hardest thing is getting the ball rolling. You must be persistent, don't give up.

'You'll hear all sorts of excuses like it's already been reduced, they're not earning any money on the item, whatever. That's the first objection, but it's not a no. What do you do then? Well, carry on talking almost as if you haven't heard what they said. Talk some more about the product, build up the rapport with the salesperson, then ask about discount again, in a slightly different way.

'Initially you could say, *I love this product, it does exactly what I need, but I don't like the price. What's the best you can do on it?* (remember to stay silent at this point) When they say that's the best price they can do, ignore it and carry on chatting. Then say something like, *You've almost sold it to me and if you can get the price down I'll go for it, if not I'll have to go elsewhere*. You'll probably get another objection. Keep talking and a few minutes later ask for a discount again in yet another way. *It's three hundred pounds. Take two hundred and I'll buy it now. Have we got a deal, yes or no?* (remember to slightly nod your head and stay silent).

'Keep pushing and don't feel embarrassed. You can be humorous, play it like a game. Sooner or later you will get a break in that salesperson. They're good at saying no, but they're not that good at saying it over and over again. It becomes slightly embarrassing for them. The second they give a penny off, they have lost the battle and that's when you go to work and build their first offer of a few quid off into a deal you'll be really happy to walk away with. You can do it because you've started the process. They are back-pedalling and you are winning.'

You may feel you lack the confidence to handle a tough haggle, but Dom's guidelines really do show the way. When school teacher Emma (from Chapter Three) first appears on *Don't Get Done, Get Dom* she avoids asking the salesperson for a discount because she is scared he will say no.

'If you don't try, you won't succeed,' Dom tells her.

Emma takes those words to heart and with Dom's help turns into a haggling champion. On her big buy she goes shopping for a new family bathroom. Dom gives Emma some excellent last-minute advice before she goes into the showroom.

'Right, you know what you've got to do,' he says. 'Get in there, get the salesperson's name, build up a rapport, work out exactly what you're buying, find out how much it is. Don't ask for a discount until we've got that price . . . then we go to work. We don't ask once. We ask twice, three times, four times . . . as many as it takes. And we keep going until we've got a price that we're happy with.'

Dom then speaks to Emma via a hidden earpiece as she talks numbers in the showroom.

Emma is in a great position to haggle. She wants several items to make up a whole bathroom suite. That means she is spending extra cash and should be able to negotiate extra discount. Having chosen the items she wants, Emma is ready to ask the total cost and start bartering on price.

Dom says, 'When he gives you the price I want you to look shocked, really horrified regardless of the price.'

Steve the salesperson says the price 'without discount' is £701.50. That's an encouraging comment because it implies there *will be a discount* as negotiations develop. Emma looks unimpressed with Steve's first offer and says nothing.

Obviously, Steve wants to make a sale, so he drops the price to £630.

Top Tip: Never accept the first offer

Dom encourages Emma to be strong and stay in control while still looking disappointed.

'I was expecting a lot less,' she tells Steve. 'So, what are we going to do?'

Emma stays silent. Steve asks what kind of deal she's looking for.

Top Tip: Make your first offer so low it's almost insulting

'Thirty-five per cent discount,' says Emma. 'That's £450.' (More than Emma expects but remember always go in low).

Steve chuckles. That's a cheeky offer, but there are no hard feelings because Emma has built up a friendly rapport. Steve says he is 'shocked', but that's all part of the game.

'The best deal we did was at Christmas and that was 20 per cent. There's no way [I can do 35 per cent]. I've got the lowest price in my head I know I can go to . . . £600, that's my limit.'

Emma still pushes for more.

'I can come up a little bit from my £450, if you can come down a lot.' (The ball is back in Steve's court. Emma is doing great. So much for his 'limit'.)

Steve drops to £560.

'You've pushed me as far as I can go,' he says.

Most of us would stop at this point, right? But Dom wants Emma to stay in the game.

'I will do £520, if you do the deal now,' she says.

Steve says Emma is a 'tough cookie' and they both laugh.

Top Tip: As Dom always says, make haggling fun!

Steve is a smart young salesperson. He knows Emma is keen to buy today and does not want to see the deal fall apart now.

'The furthest you can squeeze me down – and this is only because you're such a nice person – is £550. And that is my limit, it really is.'

But is it?

Emma goes for £540 and they finally agree to shake hands in the middle at £545. That's a saving of over 22 per cent plus free bath towels and bathroom accessories. Emma has left her bartering fears far behind her. It's hard to believe she was ever nervous. She had fun with the haggle and Steve enjoyed it too.

'That's the best discount I've ever given,' he says later. 'No customer has ever pushed me that hard before. She won't give up. She's very strong, she carried on going. I need a couple of days off, I think! She's fantastic.'

What did Emma learn from being on *Don't Get Done, Get Dom?*

'What I'll take away is that it pays to just keep going,' she says. 'When they say it's their bottom price, they don't actually mean it and they will probably go a little further.'

Dom's top tips can work for all of us.

The credit crunch means salespeople are often willing to negotiate to beat rival shops and the internet on price. There has never been a better time to find the nerve and confidence to go for that very special deal. And when you are *absolutely certain* you really do have the salesperson's 'best price', there is still one more act of the game to play . . .

Extras!

Dom says: Salespeople would rather sell at a discounted price than see you walk away having bought nothing.

CHAPTER FIVE

Extras!

'Look for things you might be able to include in the deal when the time comes.'

- When the price is right – ask for extras
- Know what you want ahead of time
- Be cheeky and have fun
- The final slap on the bum

WHEN THE PRICE IS RIGHT – ASK FOR EXTRAS

Asking for something extra as part of the deal, when you have already got the price right down, may seem like a step too far. But if you try it you will find salespeople are happy to treat this final bit of bartering as part of the game. Some shoppers are afraid that if they push too hard, salespeople will refuse to sell them the goods they want. There is no need to worry about that. Not if you do things Dom's way, as he explains.

'If you follow my guidelines of doing the deal in a polite and courteous way and build up a good rapport, nobody will ever say to you, *You can't buy that, I don't want to sell it to you. Clear off!* What you will do is reach a point where they will say, *You've got a great deal there. That's the best I can do, not a penny more. That is it*.

'Technically, that's when you have pushed them as far as you can, but I don't believe that. What they are saying is, *That's the most comfortable price I feel happy giving at this stage.* So, I always push for more.'

How do you know when a salesperson really has hit their lowest price and it's time to ask for extras?

'You can normally tell because there will be a slight change in attitude,' Dom explains. 'All of a sudden they take a harder stance on things. It's almost like they are putting their hand up and saying, *Whoa! Stop! Hold your horses! I can't do any more. I've given you a great deal. Take it or leave it*. Read the signs and get used to them. It's what you are looking for every time you go for a discount. You've done well so far, but at that stage, I ask for extras . . .'

Know what you want ahead of time

Dom's protégés on *Don't Get Done, Get Dom* are encouraged to do some research before they haggle for their big buy. It's a good idea to find out more about the product you want to buy. Make a mental note of useful extras and accessories at the same time.

'If you haven't done your research on extras beforehand, you can do it on the day,' says Dom. 'Have a look around the shop before you start the haggling process. Look for things you might be able to include in the deal, when the time comes. For example, a nice set of bath towels to go with a bathroom suite or Jacuzzi.

'Keep your extras price related. There's no point in buying a TV and getting the price right down then saying, *I'll do the deal if you throw in that top of the range music system.* It's the leads, the CDs, the smaller items, the accessories that you're looking for as extras. Have a few things in mind because you can use them to push for the best possible deal when the time comes.'

Be cheeky and have fun

The real nitty-gritty of any deal is agreeing on price. Haggling for a few extras on top is just a bit of fun. The salesperson is happy to know you are on the point of buying the goods, so throwing in a few *realistic* sweeteners is not a major problem. In fact, on *Don't Get Done, Get Dom* the salespeople often have quite a laugh with the customers at this stage.

So, be cheeky and have fun. See how much you can get within the agreed price. Landing those free extras is a nice bonus at the end of a successful haggle.

The final slap on the bum

Dom loves to go for one last extra, right at the end of the haggle. He calls it the final slap on the bum. Something silly or outrageous . . . just for the hell of it!

Let's take the example from Chapter 3 of Dom's protégé Paul whom we saw buying a caravan in *Don't Get Done, Get Dom*. Dom talks to him via a hidden earpiece and tells him to try for something extra. Paul asks for a free primus stove and the salesperson agrees. Dom then tells Paul to ask for three tins of baked beans to cook on the stove. One for each member of the family. The salesperson smiles and throws the beans in too. This is not an embarrassing attempt to get the price down further. It's all just fun from here on in.

'I remember another good story from the series,' smiles Dom. 'A lady had a downstairs toilet put in by a builder. We had a camera hidden in a Hoover while they were negotiating, before the job was done. The builder didn't have a clue what was going on. She haggled the price down and saved a lot of money. She pushed and pushed and got some other bits and pieces thrown in. In the end we had so many items thrown in by the builder, she was running out of bits to ask for, so just for fun I told her to ask for some free toilet rolls. The builder agreed. I said to her, *Make sure they're fluffy ones, not that cheap old sandpaper stuff* . . . The builder said, *Okay, I'll get you some fluffy toilet rolls. I can't do any more than that!* It was funny because she got absolutely everything she asked for and more.'

The final slap on the bum is a bonus, as long as you get your timing right.

'You've got to be careful how you ask for things and in what order,' Dom explains. 'When you go into a shop or showroom, get the price down first. That's the priority.

Then get any extras you need thrown in or heavily discounted. Push and push and push until you feel you can't go any further, then go for that final proverbial *slap on the bum*, just for the fun of it.'

Okay, you are now ready to do the deal . . .

Dom says: When I'm sure I've got the salesperson's best price, I ask for extras . . .

CHAPTER SIX

The Deal

'You've bought what you wanted at a price you were happy to pay. Now, that's a very nice feeling.'

- **Everyone's a winner!**
- **Should you feel guilty if the seller makes a loss?**
- **Good deals mean goodwill**
- **Walk out with your head held high**
- **And finally . . . Dom's message to shopkeepers**

EVERYONE'S A WINNER!

You might expect to see a bit of resentment when Dom tells salespeople he has secretly talked one of his protégés through a big buy on *Don't Get Done, Get Dom*. But time after time, the salespeople laugh it off and take it all in a good spirit.

'Every time we've done that, the shopkeepers have enjoyed it too and that's important,' says Dom. 'They've done a deal for a satisfied customer and that works for them too.'

The haggle is over, the extras are agreed. Time to shake hands on the deal and keep your end of the bargain by paying for the goods right away.

Everyone's a winner!

Should you feel guilty if the seller makes a loss?

Salespeople never sell at a loss, true?

'No, it's not actually,' says Dom. 'Salespeople might be very keen to sell you a particular product. It might be old stock and they're happy to move it. Maybe they've got to clear their warehouse and they've ordered too many of that particular item. If they're selling at a loss, they obviously have their reasons.

'It doesn't happen often. It wouldn't be a successful business if they lost on everything. So don't feel guilty if the shop makes a loss on what you buy. That's their misfortune, not yours. Bought experience is the best experience in the world. If they've paid for those goods and lost money, they won't do it again.'

Good deals mean goodwill

If you've done a deal and you don't feel good about it . . . beware!

'When you buy something you should be made to feel special,' explains Dom. 'If the whole thing has been a chore, a confrontation, imagine how awkward it will be if you have to take the product back. I wouldn't buy anything from a salesperson who didn't make doing the deal enjoyable. People like that are in the wrong job. If they don't make you feel good when you're buying, they should go and do something else where they're not face-to-face with the public.'

The salesperson's job – and it is a skill – is to do a deal that works for both parties and sends the customer away happy.

'If you're happy,' says Dom, 'the chances are you will say to your wife, girlfriend, brother, sister, aunt, uncle, next-door neighbour, *Go and see Dave at the shop down the road. Ask for a bit off. He always moans and groans, but he'll do it and he has a little chuckle. He's a nice fella*. We've all done it a million times. That's where good salespeople reap the benefit of looking after their customers and they deserve the goodwill it brings.

'If you go into a shop and buy something from a member of staff who is rude and ignorant, you will end up telling everyone you know of your experience. If your experience was that you couldn't find a salesperson, that they made it clear they weren't interested in helping you and didn't know the first thing about their products, you won't go there again. The best deals all come with the feelgood factor!

Walk out with your head held high

It's natural to feel a bit on edge when you first haggle, but if you set your mind on getting a bargain, you can do it. You really can. Dom's guidelines work time and time again. Now you can make them work for you too.

As Dom always says to his protégés: *What's the worst that can happen?*

No salesperson will throw you out for asking for discount, as long as you do it in a friendly and courteous way. Deals are there to be done, especially in the current credit crunch. Lots of salespeople enjoy a good haggle and if you get a bargain the shop wins too, because a happy customer is the best PR in the world for their business.

When you get that really good deal, the sense of satisfaction you feel is not just about the money you've saved. It is also about proving something to yourself. You've set yourself a challenge and come through as a winner. It's a major confidence boost and every time you barter for goods in a shop or showroom in future your skill will grow and grow. The more you do it, the better you get. That's the way it works.

And finally . . . Dom's message to shopkeepers

Dom says: Some shopkeepers moan at me and say, you shouldn't be telling people to ask for a discount. I ask them who their biggest competitor is now we're in the twenty-first century and often the answer is the internet. What you're up against there is someone who might not even own the product acting as a middleman. They can sell very cheaply because they have no overheads like rent, rates, heating and staff bills.

I say to shopkeepers, I'm actually doing you a favour. I'm encouraging people to come back to your shop. Shopkeepers can give something the internet can't: personal interaction. I'm saying to you, let's make people feel good about what they buy. Knock something off the price, throw in some extras, or do both. Give your customers a good feeling. Many people would rather buy things from a shop salesperson face-to-face, than from the internet. It's nice to go and see the product and have someone explain it to you. You also know there's someone there you can go and see if something goes wrong. That's the old-fashioned way of selling and it still works.

If customers ask for a discount, give it to them because if you say *No, we don't need to,* that won't buy you their loyalty. Don't live with that old-fashioned attitude of 'we give good service and a guarantee.' The goods are actually covered by the Sale of Goods Act. You're not doing anybody any favours there and the public know it. As for good service, if you don't give it you shouldn't be in business anyway! They may go and push the 'order' button on their computer and buy it cheaper elsewhere. So wake up and smell the roses. Compete with the internet. If people want some money off, give them what you can afford and make them feel good. Don't do it at cost. 'Profit' is not a dirty word. It's not about losing money, but sometimes small gestures will buy people's loyalty long term.

CHAPTER SEVEN

One-stop Guide

Haggle Like Dom – how the advice all fits together

We have looked at Dom's guidelines in detail. Now here is a quick and easy step-by-step guide to remind you of the main points to follow when going for the perfect haggle.

Research

- Budget – decide how much you want to spend
- Look for products that suit you best in your price range
- Find out how cheaply you can buy from other sources, including the internet
- Do a trial run and see how good (or bad) you are at haggling
- Ask a friend to go with you and give an honest opinion of how you did
- Have a Get Out of Jail Card ready to use if things get awkward during a haggle
- Use an excuse the salesperson can't find a way around
- Learn from your mistakes and build your confidence
- When you've done your research, get ready to haggle for real. Go for it!
- Stay cool, stay focused and make it fun. That's the perfect mindset

Winning start

- Walk into the shop, store or showroom with energy and enthusiasm
- Check out the goods on sale
- Make a note of any extras you might like to include in any deal you do
- Smile and be friendly when you start to talk to the salesperson
- Shake hands and get on first-name terms
- Get a pleasant conversation going straight away
- Crack a joke if you get the chance. Humour always helps

- Break down barriers and build rapport
- Talk about the product you are interested in but not the price

Don't haggle too soon

- Never rush to do the deal
- Let the salesperson talk about the goods they're selling
- Show you respect their knowledge
- Stay focused
- If you like the range of products on offer, say so
- If you like the shop, say so. A little flattery goes a long way
- If you don't trust the salesperson, be wary
- Don't get steamrollered into a bad buy
- Sales staff may try to sell you products that give them most commission. Don't let them. Make sure *you* stay in control
- Ask questions. How much does the salesperson really know?
- Make it clear you are not 'just looking'. You will buy today, if the price is right
- Say you can pay in the way that suits them. Cash is usually best
- Take all the time you need to decide what you want to buy
- Being flexible on product details, like colour, can save money
- When your mind is made up, it's time to haggle

Let's talk numbers

- Play it cool on price
- Never tell the salesperson your maximum budget. That's for you to know and them to guess!
- Act shocked when they tell you how much the product you want costs. Look as if you've just sucked a lemon
- Let them know you can buy it elsewhere. Name local rivals
- Show a printout from the internet with a rock-bottom price
- Give the salesperson you're talking to a chance to compete
- Be positive in *everything* you say
- Make your first offer so low it's almost insulting. But don't be aggressive when you say it
- Let the salesperson know you realise you are being a bit cheeky
- Give a little nod. Send a positive message
- Then stay silent
- Don't say a word until they speak
- They will tell you your offer is far too low
- That gives you the chance to ask the key question
- *What's your best price?*
- Now the real haggle begins
- Be ready for the salesperson to object when you ask for a discount
- Say you can come up a little, if they come down a lot
- Push, push and push for a lower price. Be cheeky and use humour
- Answer every question with a question of your own e.g. The salesperson says, *Okay, if I drop to £500, have we got a deal?*

- You then come back with an offer of your own
- *Make it £300 and I'll shake hands with you now. Okay?*
- Stay silent after every offer you make. That's how to play the game

Extras

- Make sure you really have got the salesperson's 'best price'
- Look for a slight change in attitude, a harder stance
- Then go for some free extras to be thrown in with the deal
- Have a clear idea of the extras you would like ahead of time
- Be realistic in what you ask for
- Accessories to the product you are buying are a good idea e.g. a set of towels with a bathroom suite
- When those extras are agreed, go for the *final slap on the bum*
- Ask for one outrageous final extra . . . just for the fun of it!
- Say it with a smile on your face

The deal

- Shake hands on the deal in a good spirit
- Keep your promise: buy the goods right away
- The salesperson has a happy customer and that means good PR
- You have overcome your nerves and learnt to haggle
- Walk out with your head held high
- Everyone's a winner!

CHAPTER EIGHT

Dom Classics

See how Dom's top haggling tips slot together to land amazing bargains in classic examples of two of the most popular features in the series. ***The Big Buy*** sees Dom working undercover to advise nervous shoppers on how to negotiate with sales staff and buy at the best possible price. ***High Street Haggle*** sets Dom against the clock to find a great deal. He does it every time! Enjoy these edited highlights, which provide a masterclass in how to ***Do It Like Dom!***

Dom Classics

The Big Buy – Hot Tub

This is a very good example of how controlling the situation, when dealing with a salesperson, can save thousands of pounds!

THE SET-UP

Naz wants to buy a hot tub for his partner Tina, which will help massage the aches and pains she sometimes gets as the result of a bone marrow transplant she had in her fight against leukaemia.

On the day of The Big Buy, Dom encourages Naz to stay in control when dealing with the salesperson. He reminds him to 'stick to his guns' when the time is right and also to know when to say nothing. These are crucial moments in a deal. Naz is wearing a hidden earpiece. Dom will talk him through the deal using a walkie-talkie . . .

DOM TAKES UP HIS POSITION IN A NEARBY CAR.

DOM: Alright Naz, off you go.

NAZ WALKS INTO THE HOT TUB SHOWROOM.
A SALESPERSON GREETS HIM.

NAZ: I was looking for a tub.

DOM: We haven't got this guy's name and he doesn't know

yours. Introduce yourself. Say *Hello, I'm Naz* and get his name.

NAZ: What's your name?

SALESPERSON: Alex.

NAZ SHAKES ALEX'S HAND

NAZ: Naz.

ALEX: Pleased to meet you.

Top Tip: Always get the salesperson's first name. Use it as often as you can.

ALEX SHOWS NAZ A TOP-OF-THE-RANGE HOT TUB.

DOM: Let him go through his spiel because obviously it gives him confidence and gets him a bit more relaxed.

Top Tip: Don't start negotiating too soon

ALEX EXPLAINS THE HOT TUB HAS FORTY JETS.

DOM: Forty jets? That's more than Richard Branson's got! Right Naz, if you like that one can you give me a cough?

NAZ COUGHS.

DOM: Good boy. We know which one we're going to go for.

NAZ: What kind of price are these?

DOM: Good. Don't mention discount yet.

ALEX: This as it stands is £16,600.

DOM: Trust you to go for one that's £16,600! Where did that come from? You only had 13 grand when you started!

DOM KNOWS IT'S TIME TO START HAGGLING.

DOM: Naz, I think it's time to move this up a step now. Say to him, *Okay, look, it's winter, (bad time for hot tub sales, good time for purchasers) pre-Christmas, let's talk about the price.* See if you can get him sitting down at a desk. Mention his name whenever possible as well. It's very, very good.

NAZ: Okay, Alex, can we sit down and I'll just detail what I'm looking for on this titanium model.

EXCELLENT! NAZ IS TAKING CONTROL OF NEGOTIATIONS.

ALEX: The best price I can do on that particular spa there is £12,850.

DOM: Good start, but we can do better.

Top Tip: Never accept the first offer

DOM: Look shocked and say, *That's way above my budget.*

NAZ: It's a bit over my budget. (This isn't forceful enough and the salesperson may believe they are close to Naz's ideal price)

DOM (DETERMINED): Naz, I want you to be really, really cheeky here. I want you to go in really low. Tell him, *eight thousand pounds*.

NAZ: What have you got for eight? (Naz is rather nervous and rather than try and get the price down, he is suggesting looking at a cheaper model. Never do this.)

DOM: No, no, not *what have you got for eight*. You want *this one* to start with an eight.

Top Tip: Go in with such a low offer, it's almost insulting

NAZ: Is there any chance you can go down to eight for this one? (Negative phrasing, but at least he asked)

DOM: Right, that's it. Now, don't speak, don't speak.

ALEX: I'm already down from £16,600 to £12,850, a saving of nearly £4,000.

DOM: Say, *That's a shame because this is the one I wanted and it's too dear*.

NAZ: That's a shame because this is the one I wanted.

DOM: This is part of the game, Naz. Don't be embarrassed, right?

NAZ: Unless we can get it down to a reasonable . . . well . . . (Nerves kicking in again)

DOM: A *much* lower price.

NAZ: . . . a much lower price, I might have to leave.

DOM ASKS NAZ TO SAY HE NEEDS THE PRICE TO BE 'WELL BELOW £10,000'.

DOM: Now don't speak. Stay silent.

Top Tip: Note how Dom has raised Naz's offer from that rock-bottom £8,000. While haggling you can slowly increase your offer – but still keep it low!

ALEX THE SALESPERSON STAYS CALM AND POLITE. HE KNOWS NAZ HAS EVERY RIGHT TO GO FOR THE BEST DEAL HE CAN GET.

ALEX: If potentially I could get that [price] down to say £12,000 . . .

DOM: What I want you to say to him Naz is, *Alex, go and have a word with your boss.*

NAZ LOOKS ACROSS THE SHOWROOM.

NAZ: Is that the boss? Would he allow . . .?

ALEX: I'll have a chat with him.

DOM: Remind him before he speaks to the boss, *It needs to be below ten Alex, or you can't go for it.*

NAZ: It's got to be below ten or I can't go for that one.

ALEX GOES TO TALK TO HIS BOSS. BRIEF PAUSE.

Top Tip: Always deal with the person who has the authority to give you the best possible deal

DOM: I can hear footsteps. Is he coming back?

NAZ (WHISPERS): Yeah.

ALEX SITS DOWN AT HIS DESK.

ALEX: Because that [hot tub] is in stock, the bottom line price on that spa would be £10,995 (the price keeps tumbling down).

DOM: Say, *Do you know what, that's such a shame because that's just slightly over my budget now.*

NAZ: That's over my budget.

DOM: Now don't speak.

ALEX: You've got a substantial saving.

DOM: Don't speak (psychologically, the salesperson will know he hasn't done a deal at this stage.)

ALEX: That is a very popular spa.

DOM: Say, *Ten grand's very popular as well.*

NAZ: Ten grand's very popular in my pocket as well.

DOM: Tell him to go and ask his boss again. Say, *Try one more time . . .*

ALEX: Give me a little bit for me to go back to him and say, *It's not ten grand it's* . . . (this is a game where the salesperson is finding out how much more Naz would be willing to pay. At this point, stick to your guns!)

DOM: No!

NAZ IS SO CONFIDENT NOW, HE OVERRULES DOM!

NAZ: £10,250.

DOM: Naz, you let me down.

ALEX: If you could up your offer to £10,350, I will shake your hand now.

DOM: I told you mate, you should have stuck at ten. Say *No, you've pulled me up from ten grand. There's no more money, Alex.*

NAZ: It's a stretch at ten and I've found another £250. I can't do any more.

DOM: Say, *Take it or leave it, Alex.*

NAZ: Take it or leave it.

DOM: That's it.

ALEX SAYS HE WILL NEED A 30 PER CENT DEPOSIT. NAZ SAYS THAT IS NOT A PROBLEM. NAZ THEN CONFIRMS THAT THE PRICE INCLUDES A FREE SITE SURVEY, A LID FOR THE HOT TUB, PLUS DELIVERY

AND FITTING. ALEX AGREES EVERYTHING IS INCLUDED IN THE REDUCED PRICE OF £10,250.

ALEX: Have we got a deal?

DOM: Say, *Not quite actually, there's a couple of extra things I want.*

Top Tip: When you have got the price as low as it will go, try for some free extras as part of the deal

DOM PUSHES HARD WHEN HE LISTS THE FREE EXTRAS HE WANTS FOR NAZ, TINA AND THEIR SIX CHILDREN. NAZ KEEPS A STRAIGHT FACE AS HE WRITES DOWN THE LIST.

DOM: Right, booster [seat] cushions [for the spa], eight pairs of slippers, eight bath towels, two garden plants, two garden gnomes . . . Also a little bottle of bubble bath. Now when you've done that, push the list under his nose and say, *There you go, Alex, I know I'm being cheeky but throw those in and we've got a deal.*

NAZ GIVES ALEX THE LIST.

NAZ: I know I'm being cheeky, but can you throw those in as well?

ALEX (CALMLY): Absolutely no way. Firstly, I wouldn't be able to do that spa at that price without the director.

NAZ: Where's the director?

ALEX: He's sitting there.

NAZ: Ask him to come over and I'll have a word.

DOM: Good boy Naz. Good. Here we go . . .

ALEX INTRODUCES NAZ TO JONATHAN, THE DIRECTOR. THEY SHAKE HANDS.

NAZ: We're almost there with Alex . . .

JONATHAN: Alex just asked me about booster cushions. We sell these aromatherapy ones. There's four different versions. Do a deal with me and I'll give you one of each.

DOM (TO VIEWERS): That's another 48 quid off!

DOM CUTS BACK ON HIS WISH LIST OF EXTRAS.

Top Tip: Dom knows it's time to seal this deal with goodwill on both sides

DOM: Tell him you'll settle for the slippers as well.

NAZ: Tell you what, throw the towels in.

DOM: Okay, towels, good. Now don't speak, don't speak.

JONATHAN: I'd rather give you eight [spa] oils.

DOM: All right, settle for eight oils.

NAZ: All right, eight oils then.

DOM (SMILING): Good boy. Shake his hand, shake his hand!

NAZ, ALEX AND JONATHAN SHAKE HANDS. IT'S SMILES ALL ROUND.

DOM GOES INTO THE SHOWROOM AND EXPLAINS NAZ'S HAGGLE HAS BEEN SECRETLY FILMED. ALEX LOOKS A BIT SHOCKED BUT LAUGHS.

DOM: How do you think he did?

ALEX: He beat me down to within about an inch of my life! He did the best job I can think of, of anyone who's been in here in a long, long time.

JONATHAN JOINS THEM AND AGREES NAZ HAS GOT A BRILLIANT DEAL.

JONATHAN (SMILING): He really is the winner. Absolutely, without any question.

NAZ IS ELATED.

NAZ: It was absolutely fantastic! Really enjoyed myself. I felt it was a game that was being played. I just cannot believe I've got that tub for that price.

Naz has saved £6,350. That's over 38 per cent discount. Right from the start of the haggle, he took control and had fun negotiating his Big Buy.

Dom Classics

High Street Haggle – Furniture Shops

When it comes to haggling, Dom's advice is clear. Never give up!

THE SET-UP

Emma is shopping for sofas. She has a new flat and needs seating for four people. Her maximum budget is £1,000. Emma admits she would not bargain over the price. Dom wants to prove that you can get discounts on goods if you are prepared to haggle. He has just one hour to do it. Dom uses a hidden camera so shops are not aware he is filming. (It's worth noting that when this was filmed, Dom was not as well known as he is now.)

Dominic follows three of his top haggling tips:

1. Deal with the person who can give a discount.
2. Be flexible about product details, e.g. colour of sofas.
3. Never accept the shop's first offer on price. Keep pushing for the best you can get . . . then go for some extras, just for the fun of it!

First shop:

Dominic sees two sofas for £1,220. He offers £700 for the two.

Top Tip: Always go in with a very low first offer

The salesperson says he will take £1,040 for the two. That's about 15 per cent off. Dom asks to speak to the boss who says £1,040 is 'absolutely my best price'. Dom leaves to try elsewhere.

Second shop:

Forty minutes left. Dom is offered two sofas for £1,077 each. Dom thinks this is 'far too dear'. What about a discount? The shop offers £899 per sofa. Dom tries for £500 each. The salesperson says no. Dom leaves, but is still determined to do a deal for Emma. Time for one last shop . . .

Third shop:

Twenty minutes left. Dom sees two sofas at £650 each. Total price £1,300.

This time his top three tips fall into place:

1. He is dealing with a salesperson who can give discounts.
2. Dom is flexible on colour and style.
3. He keeps pushing for the best and final offer, with some extras!

Dom offers £800 for two sofas. The salesperson says he can have them for £900. That's £400 off but Dom keeps bartering. He says his best offer is £800, but he will pay any way the shop wants. The salesperson tries for £850, but finally agrees to sell the sofas for £800. That's a total saving of £500! Dom even gets a mattress protector thrown in on the deal . . . just for the hell of it! Salespeople will quite often try to meet you in the middle of your price and theirs. It's a sort of goodwill gesture. Don't give in and stick to your guns because quite often you will win.

Dom hurries back to meet Emma just in the nick of time. His hour is up, but he's had a real result. Emma is delighted when she hears Dom has saved her £500.

'It's a massive saving,' she says. 'I would have paid £1,300.'

Back at the shop, the salesperson says Dom was very charming. 'A bit pushy but he's got away with a very good deal. A brilliant deal.' The salesperson's smile on camera says it all. He knows he met his match on this Dom Classic!

Dom Classics

The Big Buy – Petra's Business Haggle

Petra is a business woman and she needs advice on how to get really good deals when she is working.

THE SET-UP

Petra turned her back on corporate business to build herself a career in interior design and property renovation. Petra has always had a flair for design and really enjoys her new life, but she is keen to get Dom's advice on how to get the best price when buying materials for her building projects.

'I need to get better at getting good deals for what I do,' says Petra. 'So whatever I purchase I get at the best possible price.'

Dom is more than happy to give advice that will help her in her career. His first assignment is to help her buy some trendy wooden decking for the flat she is currently renovating. Petra knows exactly what she wants: a chic, modern, young, urban feel.

'I've been doing deals since I was knee-high to a grasshopper,' says Dom. 'I'm sure I can get Petra the deal she needs and teach her some top tips that will help save serious money in the future.'

What is Petra like at haggling?

'I always ask for discount,' she says, 'but if I get quite an adamant no, I will probably back away.'

Petra agrees when Dom says she gives up too easily.

'There's always room for improvement, so I'd like to get better at it.'

Petra does a trial run on trying to get a bargain at a garden centre so Dom can see her in haggling action. Things don't go too well and afterwards the salesperson gives his verdict. 'She was quite an easy customer to deal with. She gave up on negotiation quite quickly. She certainly wasn't pushing and I wasn't prepared to give a discount unless she was [pushing].'

Petra is realistic about how she did. 'I enjoyed it . . . didn't do very well though.'

Dom sums things up. 'Petra, I'm going to sound like your old headmaster and say, *could do better*.'

'I'm sure I could,' Petra agrees and when it comes to her real Big Buy, she does just that. A lot of the secret filming for the show takes place in shops and showrooms, but this time it's an open-air haggle. Petra has invited two builders to the back garden where she wants the decking laid. Dom will be inside the house giving her advice on a walkie-talkie.

Dom gives Petra some last-minute tips, just before the men arrive.

'Let them measure up. Tell them exactly what you want so there's no confusion later on. Then we go to work on the price. But don't ask them initially for a discounted price or their best price. The reason being, at least we'll know what they start at and how much discount we are actually getting.'

The scene is set for Petra to haggle like never before . . .

TWO BUILDERS ARRIVE. PETRA GREETS THEM AT THE FRONT DOOR.

PETRA: Excellent timing! Are you Steve?

STEVE: Yes.

PETRA: Hi, nice to meet you.

STEVE: This is my partner Jay.

PETRA: Jay, nice to meet you. Come on in.

STEVE: He's the Kiwi, I'm the Aussie.

PETRA SMILES AND GUIDES THEM OUT TO THE BACK GARDEN.

DOM (TO VIEWERS): Remember, the three tips Petra needs to use here are:

1. Build a rapport before she asks for a discount
2. She must not take the first offer they make her
3. And if she can't get a serious discount out of one of the guys, she should play one colleague off against the other

SECRET CAMERAS PICK UP THE ACTION WHEN STEVE AND JAY HAVE MEASURED THE GARDEN AND WORKED OUT A PRICE FOR THE WORK.

PETRA: Are you done?

STEVE: Pretty much. The hardwood decking without lights will be £2,500.

DOM (TO PETRA VIA EARPIECE): Don't comment on that. Just look disappointed.

PETRA: And how much was the softwood?

STEVE: £2,300.

DOM: Now I want you to say, *Guys, I've got to be honest, you're very very expensive compared to other people.*

PETRA: I have to tell you this is very expensive compared to what I've had.

DOM: A thousand pounds cheaper on both of them (hardwood and softwood).

PETRA: They said £1,300, supplied and fitted.

STEVE: I don't know where they're getting their timber from. Whether they're paying for it or not. There's no way. Our materials alone . . . (She has gone in very low, just like in the training. Great!)

DOM: Now what you're going to do in a second is say, *All right guys, give me your best price.* And then we'll see what they come down to.

PETRA: Okay, give me your very best price. See what that comes to.

STEVE: We'll try and be here for two days . . .

PETRA: I like the grafting bit. I'll get you lots of tinnies. (LAUGHS)

DOM (SMILING TO VIEWERS): She says these cheeky remarks, then laughs at the end of it, which is good.

STEVE AND JAY ARE STILL THINKING ABOUT THE PRICE.

PETRA: Shall I give you another five minutes between yourselves?

STEVE: Just a minute or two.

PETRA: I'll do that.

DOM: Pop in here for a sec.

PETRA COMES INTO THE HOUSE TO SEE DOM WHO IS HIDDEN IN A BACK ROOM.

DOM: You're doing well. I don't think we'll get a fortune off them, but we'll try.

THE ACTION CUTS BACK TO THE GARDEN.

STEVE: The best we can take off is £300.

DOM: That's a start. Tell them you can come up a bit but say, *Guys, you're going to have to help me out a little bit more here.*

PETRA: I can come up a bit guys, but you need to help me a little bit more here.

DOM: That's good, that's good. Now don't speak for a second. Let them work the price out.

STEVE: The best we can do – and we're going under the £2,000 mark then – is £1,950. That's probably *the lowest* we could go.

DOM: They keep creeping down. Every time you ask, they give you a little more off.

STEVE: £1,950 because, like we said, the most we could stretch is £50 off our labour.

DOM: Say, *I'll stretch my budget, I'll go to £1,750,* and put your hand out to do a deal and don't speak.

PETRA: I'll tell you what, I'll go up to £1,750 and we'll have a deal.

DOM: Now don't speak.

PETRA: We'll have a deal right now. (Fatal mistake. Always stay silent at this point).

DOM: No, I said don't speak.

Top Tip: Know when to stay silent in negotiations

STEVE: I don't think we could do £1,750, I really don't.

JAY: I don't think so either.

DOM: Say, *Come on, I like Australia and I like New Zealand.*

PETRA: I love New Zealand, I love Australia, go on . . .

DOM (SMILING): You are working these men!

STEVE: We can meet halfway. We're saying £1,950, you're saying £1,750. We could go £1,850?

DOM: They've dropped another hundred pounds!

STEVE: That's the bottom line, we're meeting in the middle then.

JAY: We're doing you a favour.

DOM: Now don't speak. Listen to me, don't speak at this moment. Let them talk amongst themselves.

PETRA STAYS SILENT.

STEVE: £1,800?

DOM: They've dropped now, another fifty quid.

PETRA STILL SAYS NOTHING.

STEVE: £1,750 and you supply the beers.

DOM: Say, *Okay £1,750, I'll supply the beers, but what I'd like off you guys is a little pot plant for the corner of the garden and that will make the deal.*

Top Tip: When you've got the price right down, go for some extras

PETRA: Okay, I'll supply the teas, the coffees, the tinnies, but I want a little pot plant thrown in . . .

DOM: For each corner, say for each corner. Go on, be cheeky!

PETRA (SMILING): . . . for each corner.

STEVE: Each corner?

JAY: Each corner? No . . .

PETRA: There's only four corners.

JAY: Steve's only got one pot plant at his house.

PETRA LAUGHS.

DOM: Say, £1,750 and four pot plants and offer to shake his hand.

PETRA: £1,750 and four pot plants.

STEVE: Okay, £1,750.

PETRA SHAKES HANDS WITH STEVE AND JAY.

DOM: You have done so well. Right, tell them you've got to make a phone call.

PETRA: I've just got to make a quick phone call. I'll be right back.

PETRA COMES INTO THE HOUSE AND HUGS DOM.

DOM: Petra, what did you think of that deal?

PETRA: Fantastic.

DOM: Do you know what, every time you asked for a discount they dropped the price down, again and again, until eventually you dug your heels in and said £1,750 and do you know what . . . who won?

PETRA: I did.

With Dom's help, Petra got herself an outstanding discount. She got £750 off the original estimate of £2,500. That's a 30 per cent saving, plus four pot plants as extras. And her new-found confidence as a haggler is sure to benefit her business in the future.

Top Tip: Whether you are haggling for yourself or your business, Dom's tips will guide you through

So what did Steve and Jay make of Petra's haggling?

JAY: My first reaction was, she drives a hard bargain. She just kept going and going.

STEVE: She wasn't taking no for an answer basically.

PETRA: I don't think I would have made it there myself [without Dom] so this has been fantastic. Invaluable for me and my business.

The *Don't Get Done, Get Dom* cameras revisit Petra's garden when the decking has been laid and it's clear Steve and Jay have done a great job. Petra is all smiles.

'I'm absolutely thrilled with this deck,' she says. 'It has really exceeded my expectations. The guys have done a fantastic job. It has given me the look and feel I wanted for the place and I got it at an incredible price.'

Dom Classics

The Big Buy – Car Showroom

This is a great example of how overcoming your nerves and learning to haggle can mean a major saving.

THE SET-UP

Tom wants to celebrate his 19th birthday by buying his first car. He admits he is extremely timid and feels very nervous about haggling with sales staff for a discount. He has set his heart on a Vauxhall Corsa and has a maximum budget of £5,000.

With 15 years experience of the car trade under his belt, Dom can help Tom to get a dream deal. But first, he sets up a trial run before the main haggle. Tom goes into a car showroom on his own. Dom admits it feels like throwing Tom to the lions. The salesperson immediately takes control. Within minutes Tom has agreed a price for a Vauxhall Corsa. Luckily Dominic has warned him to use his Get Out of Jail Card to escape the pressure of a skilful sales pitch. Tom says he has to speak to his parents about the money and leaves the showroom.

A couple of minutes later, Tom meets up with Dominic and admits he was too nervous to ask the right questions. The salesperson did 99 per cent of the talking and controlled the whole situation. Tom tried to barter, asking for a full tank of petrol if he bought the car, but the salesperson changed the subject and Tom let it drop.

'That's an old trick,' Dom explains. 'Salespeople keep rabbiting away [when they don't want to answer a question] because they know a lot of people are too embarrassed to ask twice.'

The salesperson agrees that Tom was vulnerable in the showroom. 'He was a dream come true for a salesperson. If he'd had the money I'm sure he would have paid.'

Tom has a lot to learn, but the truth is he's like many of us. He is not confident about bartering with sales staff to get the best deal. But he has picked up some valuable lessons from his trial run and with Dom's help he feels ready to haggle for real.

Tom goes into a car showroom wearing a hidden earpiece. The action is filmed by hidden cameras. Dom and Tom's dad are outside in a car and can hear everything that's going on. Dom uses a walkie-talkie to talk to Tom's earpiece and guides him through the haggle.

IN THE SHOWROOM. THE SALESPERSON IS KELLY.

Top Tip: Get on first-names terms with the salesperson. Build a relationship

DOM ENCOURAGES TOM TO SPEAK UP AND BE PROUD . . . NOT SHY.

Top Tip: Be confident. Don't let the salesperson dominate

KELLY SHOWS TOM A VAUXHALL CORSA. THE SHOWROOM PRICE IS £4,995.

TOM: Looks pretty good. What do you think you can do with the price?

KELLY: How much have you got to spend then on a car?

TOM: About five thousand pounds.

DOM (IN TOM'S EARPIECE): No . . . no . . . you don't want to spend five grand. Tell her, *If you can do it for four grand I'll buy it now.*

Top Tip: *Never* tell them your maximum budget. Go in with a low offer. Ask for such a big discount it's almost insulting. They can come down on price and you can go up . . . but not too much!

TOM: If you could do it for about four thousand, I'll do a deal absolutely right now.

DOM: Now don't speak.

Top Tip: Know when to say nothing

KELLY: Four thousand? There's no way we'd be able to take it down that low. There won't be that much money in the car.

DOM: And now say to her . . . *What's your best price?*

TOM: I need to know your best price.

DOM: That's it! That's it! Be confident. *What's your best price, Kelly?*

KELLY GOES TO CHECK ON PRICE AND RETURNS.

KELLY: I've just been speaking to the garage owner and on that car we could maybe do six months tax or something like that, but we wouldn't be able to discount the price by what you're offering.

Six months tax is a very low offer. They can spot Tim is a nervous character and without Dom's help, Tom would probably have accepted this. At least Tom had gone in low with the £4k offer though!

Top Tip: Never accept the first offer

DOM: Say to her, *Can I have a word with the garage owner myself, please?*

TOM: Would it be possible to have a word with the owner?

Top Tip: Always speak to the person at the top, who can make decisions

KELLY GOES TO CHECK.

DOM: On a scale of one to ten Tom, how nervous are you?

TOM (WHISPERS): Eight.

DOM AND TOM'S DAD LAUGH IN THE CAR.

DOM: Don't panic. You've got to show confidence all the time. Don't be nervous.

KELLY RETURNS WITH THE SALES MANAGER WHO SHOWS TOM A PRICE GUIDE ON THE VAUXHALL CORSA. HE SAYS THE CAR SHOULD REALLY BE £5,500.

DOM (TO VIEWERS): It's time to put my next tip into action . . .

Top Tip: Play one dealer off against the other

DOM (TO TOM): Tell him about the one you are going to look at which is four thousand and it's done lower miles.

TOM: It's just that I've found one in Brentwood for about £4,200.

DOM (TO TOM'S DAD): Four-two? Where did the two hundred come from? I said four grand! (Tom's nerves are showing).

SALES MANAGER: I couldn't get anywhere near that price, I'll be honest with you.

DOM: He doesn't want to budge on price, so we'll try and get some extras. Say . . . *I came to you because I want a warranty as well.*

Top Tip: Always go for extras as part of the deal

TOM: I was looking for a warranty at my price as well.

SALESPERSON: If you do the deal now, I'll do the car for you for £4,650.

DOM (TO VIEWERS): He's dropped the price by £350. It's good, but I'm hungry for more. (Remember Kelly had initially only offered six months road tax, about £80 worth).

Top Tip: Don't accept the second offer either!

DOM (TO TOM): No . . . no . . . don't you agree on that. Tell him you were hoping to pay four grand. Say . . . *I can come up to £4,300.*

TOM: Say I come up to £4,300?

SALESPERSON: I can't do it mate. I've got to make money.

DOM: What you need to say to him now is . . . *Okay, final price, if you come to £4,400 I'll do a deal with you.*

TOM: £4,400?

SALESPERSON: I can't. £4,650 is absolute bottom dollar and I'll put a warranty on for you.

DOM: No, Tom, you can't do it. Say . . . *Look, I'll do the deal now, but £4,400 is all I've got with twelve months warranty.*

TOM: It's £4,400. Right now.

SALESPERSON: I can't do it. Seriously, I can't do it.

DOM: Say . . . *I can't afford any more. I'm going to have to walk away.*

Top Tip: Keep pushing hard. The salesperson is there to make as much money as possible. That's their job. Your job is to get the best deal you can!

TOM: I can't afford any more, that's the thing.

SALESPERSON: If I do it for £4,400 there's no [one year] warranty. It's three months.

DOM: Tell him you'll ring your dad.

TOM: If you can do it at £4,400 [with one] year's warranty, I'll give my dad a ring right now.

SALESPERSON: It's £4,400, or £4,650 [with one year's warranty].

DOM: Okay, shake his hand. Go on, shake his hand. Say he's got a deal [at £4,400].

TOM AND SALESPERSON SHAKE HANDS.

OUTSIDE IN THE CAR, DOM RESTS HIS HEAD ON TOM'S DAD'S SHOULDER.

TOM'S DAD: Well done, Dom. Well done!

DOM: We got six hundred quid off [Tom's maximum budget].

TOM'S DAD: That's his insurance paid on my policy, so that's great.

DOM GOES TO MEET TOM.

DOM (TO TOM): How are you feeling right now?

TOM: Brilliant!

DOM: What do you think of me – am I a baddie? (Tom's dad then tells Dom his son is 'special needs' and the experience he has just had would do him the world of good. He has never been able to stick up for himself before. Tom's dad shakes Dom's hand with appreciation.)

TOM: No, you're a goodie – but you push hard!

THE SALES STAFF IN THE SHOWROOM ARE FRIENDLY AND JOVIAL WHEN THEY REALISE THEY HAVE BEEN FILMED BY HIDDEN CAMERAS. THE SALES MANAGER ADMITS THE CAR WAS SOLD FOR ALMOST TRADE PRICE.

SALESPERSON: We tend not to discount cars to that extent, so Tom got a very, very favourable deal.

Dom Classics

The Big Buy – Laptop computer

See how confidence can soar when you learn to relax and enjoy haggling with the salesperson.

THE SET-UP

Samantha wants to buy a laptop for her son Jack (Chapter One). She has taken a year to save £1,000 for this surprise present. Sam gathers some valuable information on a trial run. She finds out which computer will be best for Jack's needs, at school and at home. The laptop should cost around £500, leaving plenty of money to buy equipment and extras.

She knows what she wants and how much it should cost. That is an excellent start to any Big Buy, but Sam is still nervous about haggling. Dom meets her before she goes shopping and promises that buying the laptop will be fun. Sam looks a bit on edge, but Dom will be passing on his advice, via a walkie-talkie, during the haggle. That's sure to help.

Sam forgets her nerves the moment she walks into the computer shop. Right from the start, she looks confident. Sam asks the salesperson's name. It's Paul. He confirms the laptop Sam wants is £499. When Paul says the laptop has a diamond screen, Sam jokes: 'I like diamonds, they are a girl's best friend, aren't they!' (Nice banter!)

Top Tip: Get to know the salesperson. Ask their name. Have a laugh. Make a friend – not an enemy

Sam confirms the computer will do everything Jack needs,

then asks about a printer and a case. Her confidence is now sky-high and she adds more and more extras to the deal. The price drops six times during the quick-fire negotiations and Sam finally lands a terrific package of goodies worth £665 for the bargain price of just £545.

She gets a laptop computer; a carry case; a printer and scanner; ink cartridges; a USB cable; a USB memory stick; a webcam; an extension mouse; 50 blank DVDs, plus extra software. The deal is sealed with a friendly hug. Dom is really impressed by how well she has done. When they first met, Sam said she would never dream of asking for a price cut or free extras.

Well . . . just look at her now!

Dom goes into the computer shop with a film crew and admits to salesperson Paul he's been helping Sam.

DOM: How do you think she's done?

PAUL: Very well.

DOM: Could she have pushed it any further?

PAUL: No, honestly.

Paul is not grumpy about the great deal Sam's got. In fact, he is very friendly, all smiles. After all, he's made a profit too. That's what good salespeople are there to do!

'It felt good,' Sam tells Dom. 'It just shows you *can* haggle and I never thought I could. So, I am quite chuffed with myself. Dom gave me the confidence and I think I can go out there and do it on my own now.'

And if Sam can do it, you can too. This Dom Classic proves the point . . .

Dom Classics

High Street Haggle – Express Masterclass

Dom advises his *Don't Get Done, Get Dom* protégés to take their time when they are haggling. But when he is up against the clock in the series, Dom has the chance to show his experience and get deals done in a hurry. He will haggle for anything . . . anyway, anyhow, anywhere.

The flower seller

Dom proves you can negotiate even on low-priced items. Dom meets a flower seller and admires her street stall. He introduces himself with a smile and a joke and asks her name. It's Terri.

Top Tip: Even in a quick haggle, Dom asks for a first name and builds rapport

Dom asks how much a bunch of lilies will cost. Terri says £22. Dom keeps his cheeky smile and asks for her best price. Terri says £20. Dom's sure she can do better.

Top Tip: Never accept the first offer

Terri drops the price to £19. Dom's still not buying.

Top Tip: Don't accept the second offer either!

TERRI: That's good for me. I don't usually give anything. You're lucky because you're being nice.

DOM: I'm always nice because it gets you places.

Dom keeps chipping away. Terri finally drops the price to £18.

Deal done!

The dentist

Dom is always keen to show viewers you really can haggle for anything if you have the nerve. Would you dream of bartering with a dentist? Dom does just that and extracts a great deal.

He walks into a high-street dentist and asks the receptionist about teeth whitening.

The course normally costs £550, but is on offer at £450. Dom politely asks if he can speak to the dentist in person, then tells him he doesn't want to spend more than £350. The dentist only hesitates briefly before saying okay to Dom's offer. That's a £200 saving!

'Whoever would have thought you could negotiate with a professional person like a dentist?' says Dom. 'But I can negotiate with anybody and that dentist didn't even mind. I got £550 worth of treatment down to £350 and they [dentist and assistant] are all smiles . . . like me!'

The message is clear: never say never.

The tattoo artist

Here is another example of how you can haggle for the least likely things.

Dom decides to see what price he can get on a tattoo . . .

just for the hell of it. After chatting to a receptionist in the tattoo parlour, Dom asks to speak to the tattoo artist in person.

Top Tip: Always speak to the person who can make decisions on discounts

Chris the boss tells Dom the tattoo he has chosen will cost £300.

Dom asks for his best price.

Chris drops to £250.

Dom offers £150.

Chris says if Dom has it today, he'll do it for £150.

The price has been cut in half in seconds.

Shame Dom didn't really want the tattoo. At that price though, it was a bargain!

The camping equipment shop

Dom is looking for a three-man tent. He quickly gets on first-name terms with Joe, the young salesperson. Joe has the tents in stock and says they are 'quite cheap' at £40. Dom's not rushing to buy at that price, so Joe offers to do the online price 'which will be slightly cheaper'.

Dom thanks him for the internet price but says what he didn't like was the word 'slightly'.

Joe laughs. He and Dom have built up a friendly rapport.

Joe looks up the online price on his computer. It's £33.99.

Dom says it's an odd figure.

JOE: £30?

DOM: £25 and we've got a deal.

Joe checks prices on his computer again.

JOE: Okay, £25!

Another super-fast deal reaches a successful conclusion.

The camera shop

Dom is shopping for a camera. He sees the one he wants in a shop for £700.

Dom asks what they can do on price and the shop comes down to £640.

Dom explains he has seen that camera cheaper online, but he would prefer to buy it from a local retailer and use a local shop.

Top Tip: Let salespeople know they have rivals

Immediately the salesperson offers the camera for £610.

Dom says if he gets 20 per cent off he'll buy it today.

Top Tip: Let the shop know you're not a time waster. You mean business!

Dom always advises *Don't Get Done, Get Dom* viewers to

speak to the boss where possible, i.e. the person who can approve a discount. The camera shop salesperson explains his boss is out. Dom asks to speak to him on the phone. It may seem cheeky, but the salesperson makes the call and seconds later Dom gets his wish.

Dom explains to Jazz, the owner, that the camera is cheaper on the internet, but he'll buy it for £540 today.

Jazz says okay!

Dom then follows his own guidelines and gets to work on getting some extras as part of the deal and ends up with £160 off (12 per cent discount) plus a free box of 10 recordable DVDs. (The proverbial slap on the bum).

An Express Masterclass in minutes.

Dom meets his match

And finally, some quick-fire humour!

Jackie needs a car stereo. She agrees to give Dom an hour to find a great deal. Dom asks her to wait for him in a coffee shop and says he's buying the coffee. Normally at this stage of the show people just say thanks, but Jackie is up for a bit of light-hearted banter!

JACKIE: Throw in a bacon buttie and you might have yourself a deal.

DOM: I'm saving you money and you want a buttie as well?

JACKIE: Yes!

DOM (SMILING): I like your cheek! I'll tell you what, I'll pay for the bacon, you pay for the bread roll. How's that?

JACKIE: All right then!

One hour later Jackie is smiling again when Dom tells her he has got her a top deal in a local shop. Her car stereo has dropped from £200 to £147.50. That's over 25 per cent discount.

JACKIE: That's superb!

Dom's reward – a kiss from Jackie.

The surprise bacon buttie barter may have ended with honours even, but when it comes to those high street haggles, Dom is definitely in a class of his own . . .

Dom Classics

The Big Buy – Double Glazing

Dom's haggling tips can land great deals in shops and showrooms, but they can work just as well when you need work done on your home.

THE SET-UP

Roger is a student living in Preston. Instead of paying rent through his college years, he has bought a house with his friend Henry. They want double glazing to improve the property for themselves and their flatmates. Roger spent a year living in China as part of his university course. He did some bartering in Beijing, but never in the UK. Why? He says because the culture is different. Brits don't ask for a good deal, they just accept the price. Now Roger needs a great deal on eight double-glazed windows and a back door, so it's time to sharpen up his act. Dom knows it won't be easy.

'Double-glazing salespeople are among the shrewdest and best around. The competition is immense. It's a very, very big game. But if you play it right you can save a lot of money.'

Dom sends Roger on a trial run to buy some Chinese cooking equipment. The salesperson has been primed by Dom to make it difficult for Roger to get a deal. So, it is a tough test.

Roger listens politely as the salesperson goes into great detail on the various items for sale.

When Dom reviews the trial run on DVD, he has some advice for Roger.

'There's a lot of waffle [from the salesperson], which is

quite nice. It's conversational, which I like, but you must not get confused by waffle. When the time's right, and you'll know when that is, you need to get back to the point in question. And that is, how much are the goods you're buying? *Let's have a deal. Let's talk about it now . . .'*

Top Tip: Don't get sidetracked. Get down to the nitty-gritty when the time is right

The salesperson tells Roger the cooking equipment is £30.91. Roger asks if he would be able to knock anything off. Dom stops the DVD.

'You've said to that guy, *Would you be able to knock any money off?*' says Dom. 'What are the two possible answers that can come back from that question.'

'Yes or no?'

'Exactly, you've hit the nail on the head,' Dom agrees. 'Yes or no won't get you a discount. You have to ask the question in a way that the salesperson will have to respond without just saying yes or no. You could say, *If I buy that today what is your best price?*'

Roger keeps trying for a discount, but at the end of the trial run Simon the shopkeeper feels he could have been more forceful. 'He didn't haggle hard enough' is his verdict.

Roger is determined to do better when the time comes to face the double-glazing salesperson. Dom's team will be filming the action at his house on secret cameras. Roger wears a hidden earpiece so he can hear Dom's advice, from a nearby car, all through the haggle. Henry, who co-owns the house, is on hand to see how Roger gets on. He says Roger is basically 'timid, kind and thoughtful'.

'I'm going to ask him to be someone he's not,' Dom tells Henry. 'I'm going to take him out of his comfort zone and he's going to have to do that if he wants to save any money.'

Roger looks nervous before his Big Buy, but snaps into action when he greets the salesperson at his front door. He gives him a warm welcome and gets straight on first-name terms. Billy the salesperson measures the windows in every room, then it's time for a quote.

Billy says the eight windows will cost £2,793.

ROGER: How much would it be with the door?

BILLY: £3,366.

DOM (TO HENRY IN CAR): Shall we go for it with the door or without the door?

HENRY: Go with the door, if we can.

DOM: Right, Roger, Henry said we'd like to go for the deal with the door.

ROGER: I would like to have the door done as well, but I just can't afford that price.

BILLY: So you're negotiating with me now?

LAUGHTER.

BILLY: What was your budget?

DOM: Tell him, *I'm looking to spend no more than two grand*. Call his bluff. (TO HENRY) Ouch! That will hurt him.

Top Tip: Never tell the salesperson your maximum budget

ROGER: I'm looking to spend around two grand.

BILLY: Two grand? No.

DOM: This is good. Just stay silent for a minute. (After a slight pause, the salesperson is the next to speak.)

BILLY: The absolute lowest I can do is £3,058 and that's absolute bottom.

Top Tip: Never accept the first offer

DOM: Just say, *I'm really sorry, Bill, that's above my budget.*

ROGER: Yeah, that's kinda out of my budget really. It's really pushing it.

BILLY: Two and a half, without the door, is the lowest I can do.

DOM: *What about if I come up to £2,300, with the door, then I'll do a deal, but that's going to be my best offer.*

ROGER: £2,300 with the door, then I'll do a deal.

DOM: That's good. That's good.

BILLY: I had two and a half grand [as] my lowest price without the door . . .

BILLY WORKS ON SOME FIGURES ON HIS CALCULATOR AND SAYS HE CAN'T INCLUDE A DOOR FREE OF CHARGE.

DOM: Say, *All right Billy, don't worry then, I'll get the other two quotes in this afternoon and see how I get on.* (Calling the salesperson's bluff).

ROGER: Don't worry Billy, I can get a couple more quotes.

BILLY: You can do, yeah.

DOM: You've got to say to him, *Look, we keep talking, and we're beating around the bush. If you can give me a better price we'll do the deal.*

ROGER: We keep beating around the bush, but if you could just give me a better deal then . . .

BILLY: A slightly better deal?

ROGER: Yeah.

BILLY: Right, absolute bottom . . .

DOM: Still look disappointed . . .

BILLY: That's £2,900.

ROGER: Two nine?

BILLY: Two nine and that's absolutely bottom.

DOM: Say, *I'll meet you in the middle. Two seven, we've got a deal.*

ROGER: I'll come up to two seven and then we'll make a deal.

BILLY: I can't do two seven.

BILLY STAYS PROFESSIONAL AND POLITE BUT HEADS FOR THE DOOR AND WALKS OUT INTO THE STREET.

DOM: Don't worry lads, the game's not up until I say it is. (TO VIEWERS) See how he [Billy] is not racing to get in his car and drive away? The deal's not over yet.

BILLY STOPS AND LOOKS AT THE OUTSIDE OF THE HOUSE THEN TALKS TO ROGER.

BILLY: I can't even change the style [of the windows] to get it down cheaper. Let me just come back in and have a look at this, before we go our separate ways. (Billy knows he is on the verge of losing a deal here. The tables have been turned and Billy is trying one last time to get a deal done).

DOM AND HENRY ARE WATCHING AND GETTING EXCITED.

HENRY: He's going back in again!

DOM: He's a good salesperson. He doesn't want to leave. He's got as far as his car . . . This is good, he's going to come back with a slightly better price. We'll get there, we'll get there.

ACTION MOVES BACK INSIDE THE HOUSE. BILLY IS WORKING OUT SOME FIGURES ON HIS CALCULATOR.

BILLY: £2,839.

DOM: We're getting closer. Tell him, £2,800 take it or leave it.

ROGER: If we round it to two eight?

BILLY HOLDS OUT HIS HAND. THEY SHAKE HANDS.

ROGER: Deal!

DOM (TO HENRY): Two eight!

HENRY: Yes. Come on!

Billy recognises Dom when he goes into the house to explain the haggle has been filmed for TV and the air turns blue for a while. But only in jest and Billy soon calms down and gives his opinion on how Roger did in the negotiations.

'He was superb, knocked me right down.'

This Dom Classic proves Dom's top tips don't just work in shops and showrooms. You can use them anywhere.

Dom Classics

High Street Haggle – Persistence Pays

Dom proves that perseverance is the name of the game when chasing a top deal. If at first you don't succeed . . .

THE SET-UP

Dom is in determined mood for this haggle. He is in London's Charing Cross Road, which is famous for its music shops. Dom knows that where there's competition between shops, there's also a good chance of bagging a bargain. But most Brits wouldn't dare ask for money off in the high street. Dom confirms this when he asks some passing shoppers a leading question: *Would you dream of asking for a discount?* The replies are all negative.

'No!'

'Usually I don't, no.'

'I think the price is what it says in the shop. That's what you tend to pay, really.'

Many of us feel the same way, but not Mr Littlewood!

'Pay the shop's asking price?' he asks. 'Do me a favour.'

Dom is on a mission to prove he can get a great deal for a complete stranger, in just one hour. He has no idea what he will be asked to buy, but that does not faze him. He stops a young musician called Andy, who says he is looking for a Fender Jazz Bass guitar to use for teaching. Dom always says you'll get a better deal if you are flexible on things like the colour of the item you are buying. But in this case Andy knows exactly what colour he wants: sunburst yellow.

Andy goes to a local coffee shop and Dom sets off on his 60-minute mission.

'Now electric guitars can mean big bucks,' Dom tells the *Don't Get Done, Get Dom* viewers. 'Over the years the more unusual ones have become collectors' items. Eric Clapton once sold one for $959,000. Obviously, Andy isn't looking to spend quite that much. The model he's after retails at around £480 and although I can't play a note, I'm confident I can get a great discount.'

Dom plans to follow three of his top tips:

1. Build up a rapport with the salesperson because it breaks down a lot of barriers.
2. Don't take the first offer of a discount as the only offer. Push for even more.
3. Play one shop off against the other.

Secret cameras focus on the action. None of the shops know they are being filmed.

Dom always says it pays to be persistent when you are haggling. His advice: never give up. In this classic assignment he proves he not only talks the talk . . . he walks the walk!

Haggle 1:

Dom starts by asking the salesperson a cheeky question.

DOM: There's about twenty shops down here [Denmark Street]. Which one will give me the best deal on a guitar?

SALESPERSON: Depends what you're buying, really. What you'll probably find is one of them will give you a price and the others will match it. That'll be about it.

Not the most encouraging news, but Dom's not discouraged. He moves on with every intention of checking things out for himself.

Haggle 2:

Dom instantly finds a more positive salesperson. She shows him a black Fender Jazz Bass which her shop usually sells for £459. She offers it to Dom for £379, an £80 saving.

A good offer, but Dom's hungry for more.

Haggle 3:

Dom tells this salesperson he has seen the guitar on the internet for just over £300, but explains he is looking to spend 'in the low two hundreds'.

Top Tip: Make your first offer so low it's almost insulting

The salesperson asks for five minutes to see what he can do. Dom waits for his offer.

SALESPERSON: Lowest of the low would be £350.

Dom looks shocked.

The salesperson then offers to throw in a guitar bag 'to sweeten the deal', but Dom still pushes for a better price.

SALESPERSON: £340.

DOM: I really didn't want to spend more than £300. You've gone down to £340. Meet me in the middle – £320 – and I'll shake hands.

SALESPERSON: I can't do it. £340 is the bottom I can go.

Dom doesn't argue. He leaves with a smile and a handshake. He has got the guitar down to £340 and the salesperson has offered a free set of strings and a guitar bag. Not bad, but there are more shops to try.

Haggle 4:

In this shop the salesperson would need to place a special order for the bass guitar as it's not in stock. Dom says he'd be interested if the price is good enough, but it's not so he quickly moves on. Time is running out fast . . .

Haggle 5:

Dom is shown a Fender bass priced at £399. The salesperson says she'll try and do him a better deal than that. She punches some figures into her calculator.

DOM: Can you just use the minus button on that one?

SALESPERSON: Yeah, I'd like to.

A nice bit of banter, but the price doesn't drop enough and Dom's soon back on the street.

Haggle 6:

Dom tells the salesperson the best deal he has been offered so far.

DOM: I can get it for £340, free gig bag, free set of strings.

SALESPERSON: That's ridiculously cheap already.

DOM: Is it really? I was hoping to break the £300 bracket.

SALESPERSON: There's no way I can do it. [I can't] go ten, twenty quid lower than that. It's literally going to be by a pound.

DOM: Okay, thanks.

Dom leaves the shop on a friendly note and updates the viewers on his quest.

DOM: He'll give me a pound off just to get the deal. These shops are all in the same street and in direct competition, so I'm going to make the most of that by playing one off against the other.

Haggle 7:

Dom heads back to the shop that has offered the guitar for £340. He is soon having a laugh and joke with the salesperson about the music shops he has visited.

DOM: You all just play off each other which is quite crafty. I like it, I admire it.

The salesperson laughs.

Top Tip: Use humour to build that all-important rapport

Dom asks what the best price would be, if the deal is done today. The salesperson checks and comes down to £300 with the free extras. That's another price drop of £40. A great result, but the guitar on offer is black and Andy asked for sunburst yellow.

Time is virtually up, but Dom shows persistence by dashing back to the shop that offered to beat his previous best offer of £340 by just one pound to land the deal. That's the shop that has the guitar Andy wants and Dom's determined to land the best deal of all there. He's still pushing hard and enjoying the thrill of the chase.

Top Tip: Be persistent – push, push, push!

Haggle 8:

DOM: I'm feeling lucky, so I'm going back over the road [to the shop] where I built rapport earlier to give it one last push.

The salesperson greets Dom with a smile.

DOM: This time we do a deal if the price is right, yeah?

SALESPERSON: Okay.

DOM: Now, you are in competition with the other shop. We want the sunburst with a Fender bag. But you can take my word for it, it's a very, very good price [the other shop has offered].

The salesperson says he can do it for £359 and he will throw in a better quality guitar bag that costs £60, as part of the deal.

DOM: It's far too dear. I'm looking to spend three hundred quid. I've got a good deal already. You've got to better that for the deal today.

SALESPERSON: You're going to buy it now?

DOM: Right now.

SALESPERSON: Only for you, I'll do £319 including the bag.

DOM: Deal!

Dom's a happy man and so is Andy when Dom tells him the deal he has got on the sunburst yellow Fender Jazz Bass guitar of his dreams. Andy thought he might have to pay £480, but with hard work and sheer persistence Dom has got that down to £319. That's an incredible one-third off!

'That's a great deal,' smiles Andy. 'I owe you a drink.'

Cheers Dom!

PART 2

•

How To Battle Bureaucracy

CHAPTER NINE

How To Deal With Red Tape

Trying to cut through the bureaucracy of red tape can be frustrating. But on *Don't Get Done, Get Dom*, the ground rules always stay the same.

- **The squeaky wheel gets the oil**
- **Be firm, be adamant**
- **Three sides to every argument**
- **When the going gets tough**
- **Know your rights**
- **Find the weakness in their armour**
- **Overcoming barriers**
- **Call centres**
- **A chain of numbers**
- **Build a chain of information**

THE SQUEAKY WHEEL GETS THE OIL

Many of Dom's guidelines for dealing with bureaucracy in its various forms are similar to those he uses when teaching people to haggle. But in the Consumer Advice section of *Don't Get Done, Get Dom,* the guidance given has a bit more edge. Getting discount in a store is one thing, cutting through red tape or getting a substantial refund for shoddy goods or workmanship is in a tougher league entirely.

Dom has sorted out a wide range of problems in the series. He will be sharing all that experience with you in this section of the book and giving clear guidelines you can learn from and follow. When it comes to disputes of any kind, his approach starts with a simple catchphrase.

'The squeaky wheel gets the oil.'

What does he mean by that?

'If you imagine a piece of machinery with loads of cogs all working at the same time, if one of them starts to squeak that is the one the engineer is going to give the drop of oil to,' Dom explains. 'It's the same with companies and organisations. There might be scores if not hundreds of people all with similar problems. Who's going to get the attention? The one who takes the time to phone up or write a letter of complaint. The one who takes things further and doesn't accept a fob-off as an answer. That's the person who will eventually get their problem resolved because the company will want to get that monkey off their back. So that's what it means, the squeaky wheel gets the oil. Don't give up, be persistent. Keep squeaking.'

Be firm, be adamant

You must be firm when you present your complaint, but it pays to avoid confrontation.

'That's totally my style,' says Dom. 'I say be firm, be adamant, be tenacious, but with some people that turns into aggression. This negative energy will not help resolve a situation. You need to state your case and keep a level head. Some people can only do it by screaming and shouting. It's far better to channel all your aggression into determination and try not to offend people. I always set out to be firm and courteous and to give people the chance to resolve situations.

'The truth is that Brits don't like complaining. It's the same sort of feeling they have about haggling: it takes them out of their comfort zone. They build up so much fear and aggression inside them before complaining about something, they burst into this torrent of abuse as soon as they start speaking. I had a lot of people shouting and swearing at me when I was in the motor trade. They didn't have to behave like that. If they had a problem with their car, I had every intention of getting it sorted right away. But people get so worked up about complaining they go straight into an aggressive mode.

'There's another old saying I use. You've got two ears and one mouth, so you're designed to do twice as much listening as talking. I've always believed that. Swearing and shouting at people is stupid and, to a certain extent, ignorant. Things go wrong with cars, washing machines, whatever – it happens. So why not give the people a chance to sort the problem out, before slagging them off for a simple hiccup? Be courteous: firm and polite. It's easier to be nice. It's harder to be horrible. That's a good philosophy.'

Three sides to every argument

Whether chasing a refund for people who have been shabbily treated or cutting through red tape to sort out a bureaucratic wrangle, Dom always keeps an open mind when going to work on *Don't Get Done, Get Dom.*

'There are three sides to every argument,' he explains. 'There's yours, theirs and the truth. Everybody tends to bend the rules, lie a little bit about their side of things, exaggerate their stories, whatever it might be. So although you must be firm, you've got to cater for that flexibility that allows you to see the other person's side too. You need to find the middle ground. Three sides to every argument. I have that in mind every time I take on someone's problem.'

When the going gets tough

Dom may go into the disputes he deals with on the programme with an open mind, but when he finds himself facing a wall of cold indifference or angry confrontation, that's when his determination kicks in with a vengeance.

'I sometimes get lengthy and quite aggressive phone calls. All that does is start my engine up. It gets me going and the nastier someone gets, the more the nitrous oxide kicks in and I think right, I'm running at full speed now. Some people I have approached about a problem have said, *Okay, Dominic, I'll sort it out for you. I don't want any aggravation; get off my back*. We've resolved things with the minimum of hassle. But if people want to be nasty and play hardball, I'm ready for them because I'm fairly good at that. I'm very tenacious and that's when I think, *I will make it my duty, every morning I get up, to get you to resolve this. And the longer you take, the happier I'm going to feel at the end of it.*

'A lot of the cases I deal with reach a nasty, bitter stage. And I quite often end up getting quite threatening on the phone with people. Not in a way where I'm shouting and screaming, *I'm going to come down and beat you up,* but in a way where I let them know exactly what I'm going to do within the law and always within the law. I tell them the hard facts and it's a huge wake-up call for them. When I end up having to deliver my sermon that way to them it's frightening, because they can tell by my voice there's passion in what I say and what I do. So, learn to channel all your aggression into determination.'

Know your rights

Before going into any dispute it is vital to know your rights. Otherwise you might be wasting your time and energy on a battle you can never win.

'It's easy to say *know your rights,*' says Dom, 'but if you don't really know them, or you're not sure, research them. You've got organisations that can help such as Citizens Advice Bureau (www.citizensadvice.org.uk), Consumer Direct (www.consumerdirect.gov.uk) and the Office of Fair Trading (www.oft.gov.uk). The OFT don't normally deal with people direct, but they do take on some cases. All those agencies are there, and they don't cost you anything. You can also use the Which? Legal Service (www.whichlegalservice.co.uk) which will involve a small legal fee.'

Where else can you get help?

'Quite often people don't realise they've got the use of a solicitor included in their home insurance. If you've got buildings or contents cover, quite often you have legal help there with the free advice of a solicitor. You phone them up, tell them about your problem, they'll advise you on what to do. You can also research your rights on the internet or at a local library.

'Knowledge will definitely empower you in a dispute. Be sure of your facts and then, if you know you are in the right, make sure you get what you want.'

Find the weakness in their armour

When you are engaged in a dispute you are determined to win, you have to look for any weaknesses that might help you to get the outcome you deserve.

'You've got to look for people's weak spots, a weakness in their armour,' says Dom. 'Put yourself in their situation and see if there are any areas you can use to your advantage. Say it's somebody who's collecting cash payments and refusing to give back some money people are entitled to. Where is the chink in the armour? Where is the weakness? It's the fact they're paid cash. You can put pressure on them by saying, *I'm assuming that you have declared the cash you've received to the Inland Revenue and paid your tax and VAT on that?*

'If it's a person who ducks and dives a bit in life, you may hear a wobble in their voice, because nobody who's on the wrong side of the law wants the Inland Revenue on their back. So at that point their ears will prick up and they will start listening to you. They will realise you're not going away. That's what I do on the programme. I let the people I'm up against know I'm going to become the biggest pain in their life until the dispute is sorted out. That's what you've got to look for: the chink in someone's armour.'

Overcoming barriers

When dealing with bureaucracy, you must be ready to overcome barriers. They are part and parcel of most of the disputes Dom tackles in the series.

'Hitting a barrier doesn't mean the end of what you're trying to achieve,' Dom explains. 'This is where you have to show the persistence and determination we've been talking about. You can go under, over or round a barrier. You just need to find the best way of doing it.

'I remember one case in *Don't Get Done, Get Dom* where I was taking on an energy company and all the barriers were put up against me. My calls weren't answered, my emails weren't answered, my faxes weren't answered and when I phoned up the switchboard, this company had what was called a no name policy. Now a lot of companies have this and it's really, really frustrating. If you phone up and say you'd like to speak to the CEO, the person on the switchboard will ask you the CEO's name. If you don't know it, they won't put you through.

'You then ask for the person's name so you can write to them, and the switchboard operator says if you don't know, we're not telling you. Then you ask if you send a letter addressed to "The CEO", will it get to them? No, it won't; not unless you know their name and put it on the envelope. It's pure bureaucracy and you end up going round in circles.

'In this particular case they kept trying to put me through to a media relations man, but he wasn't returning my calls. I was banging my head against the wall. I had literally gone down every avenue and couldn't get to speak to anyone in authority about quite a serious issue. When you are in that situation you've got to remember, it's not a dead end. Find a way forward.

'So I stood back and thought, Okay, where's the weakness in your amour here? You've got an impenetrable system here in this country but hang on, this is a French-based company. So I then went at it from a completely different angle and got the head office number in France. I phoned and I asked to speak to the CEO and was immediately put through because they have a different policy over there. I spoke to the top cheese in France and he was so polite and courteous. He gave me all the details for the CEO in this country, name, email, direct dial number and the PA's details too.

'Next I phoned the CEO's office here and told them about the problems I'd had and that I'd had to go via France to sort things out. From that moment onwards, things started snow-balling more and more in my favour. People started answering and listening to my calls because they realised, *This monkey's not getting off our back.* That's the way the squeaky wheel gets the oil. Squeak, squeak, squeak!

'As Brits, I think we give up too easily. We go so far, but then we can't be bothered. I'm not like that, the more barriers they put up, the harder I try. Unless you feel very passionate about something, you will be fobbed off because it's very rare that problems are sorted out initially after a first contact. You have to be very determined. Always keep your calm, always be level-headed, always keep a paper trail of everything you say, send and write. I write things down all the time when I'm working on *Don't Get Done, Get Dom.* Who I speak to, what their position in the company is, what time I've called and from which phone. The reason being, if it ever went to court, you could show your phone bill and link that to the call you made on that day. There's no disputing the date, time and length of the call and the number you rang.'

Call centres

One area of telephone bureaucracy we all have to face is dealing with call centres. They can be the bane of our lives, but they often feature in the process of sorting out disputes. What's the best way to avoid the irritation they can cause?

'Once again, it comes back to finding out the name and direct dial number for the person you are speaking to,' says Dom. 'The worst-case scenario is when you've spoken to a call centre and you have to phone again. You find yourself dealing with somebody completely different and having to give the same information all over again. You can halve your problems by getting the name and number of the person you're talking to, or the name of the person who will be dealing with your problem should it escalate. Try and get a direct dial number, rather than one of these general 0844 or 0845 numbers, which drive you really bonkers. If you can go back to that same person, as opposed to a different person every single time, it reduces that big, faceless call centre to a name and a voice. That's so important.'

A chain of numbers

'When you call big companies, quite often you have to go through a process of press one for this, press four for that, now press seven, etc. My advice is when you call them for the first time, write down the chain of numbers you need, so when you ring back the second time you just punch in the numbers as they're asked for. You don't have to listen to the whole message, which can cut the whole process down to a fraction of the time.

'If you've noted the name and direct number of the person dealing with your problem, you'll avoid that chain of numbers. You can go straight to them and then, it's back to the old process as with everything else: work your way through the complaint, be reasonable in what you're asking for, allow people to tell you their point and then try and reach some sort of middle ground where you're happy, they're happy and you end up agreeing on something.

'Worst-case scenario, if you don't agree, then you'll have to go to a trading organisation, like the Ombudsman, or the watchdogs or the regulators. Most complaints now have a process where you can complain to somebody higher up, someone independent, whoever it might be.'

Dom has another good money-saving tip for phone users.

'0870 and 0871 numbers are profit-sharing numbers,' he explains. 'The longer you're on that phone call, the more that company's earning out of you. I detest them. I actually think they should be outlawed, but unfortunately they're not. 0845 and 0844 are not profit-sharing numbers, they're local rate numbers, but you still don't get them in your call plans. You don't get them free, they cost you money, and they're an inconvenience.

'So go on to the "Say no to 0870" website (www.saynoto0870.com) and find an 01 or an 02 number you can use instead. Sometimes there are even free 0800 numbers you can use as an alternative. Dial that number. Not the 0870, 0871, 0844, 0845 numbers. Avoid those when you are phoning and complaining and the cost of the whole process will be a whole lot less. At least the company you are complaining about are not earning a profit out of you for your call, so that's something I would highly recommend.'

Build a chain of information

Finding a way through the bureaucracy people at big companies and organisations sometimes hide behind can be very frustrating. For example, when people promise to call you back and never do.

'What you need to do is work your way up the chain,' says Dom. 'When you first make any sort of contact with any company, regardless of how junior the person is you're speaking to, always get their name, because if things don't move forward there's a person you can complain to. If you don't do that, the person you're speaking to may promise to look into your complaint and say they will call you back, but never do it. If you don't know their name, what can you do? They'll just ignore you. The second you have someone's name, everything will change from that moment onwards.

'If they don't do what they've promised, you can chase them up. That's what I do. *Teresa Smith? It's Dominic Littlewood. You promised me a call back and I didn't get it.* By going back to the same person, you're now becoming that squeaky wheel again. Stay polite, but you can be a little more forceful. *Teresa, you obviously let me down last time; who's your superior, who's in charge there? Who's your team manager? Who's your team leader? Who is the CEO?* Try to get to the next person up the scale, whoever it might be.

'When they say they'll put you through say, *Hang on, who are you putting me through to? Dave Smith? Right, can you give me his direct dial number as well?* You now have a different name, different number. Document all the information you're getting. Keep a list of phone numbers. You spoke to Teresa Smith, the telephonist. You then speak to Dave Smith: he's the team leader. If the chain starts breaking down and people aren't returning calls, you go back to that last person in the chain, Dave Smith. *I was promised a call back, but I didn't get one.*

'And when people promise you a call, some news about your problem, tie them down to a time. Not necessarily hours and minutes, but ask when you'll be getting that call back.

Today? Morning or afternoon? This afternoon. Any idea what time? Before three or after three? Before three o'clock. Fine. Okay, Dave, I'll wait for a call back before three o'clock today. And you're tying them down. You're putting that firm pressure on people, which lets them know you're not an idiot; you're not going away.'

How does Dom document the cases he covers for *Don't Get Done, Get Dom?*

'I write everything down in a book I always carry around with me. I build up this tree of who's in charge, what their job is, what they are like as a person. Quite often I'll give them marks out of ten on whether they're polite and helpful or rude and obnoxious. What I do as well, which annoys a lot of them, is try and get their mobile phone numbers and email addresses. Sometimes I try and do it in a sort of sneaky way. I say, *Just in case you're not there and I need to get some information, have you got a mobile number I can take?* And often they're not quick enough to say they don't like giving that number out, so I get it and it's very hard for them to avoid me from that moment onwards.

'I've taken certain companies on again and again in each series. I now know who to go to directly and I ring them up. I've got their direct dial numbers, I've got the switchboard numbers, I've got their mobile phone numbers, I've got their PA's name, email address, everything. I don't just write it down on a scrappy bit of paper. I document it all in the books I use when we're making a series. Flame TV, the production company, have got those books from the first three series now. They're full of vital information.

'That's what you've got to do, write everything down, whether you are tackling a bureaucratic problem or chasing a refund. Whatever the situation is, keep a paper trail of everything that's relevant because you can use it in the future. Log dates and times of calls, what phone number you've dialled from as well, because if the people you are up against ever dispute what you are saying, you can check everything because you've been thorough. You will be able to check which phone you made a certain call from and dig out your bill. Then you can tell them, *12th March, I was on the phone for an hour and a half. That's when I called and spoke to you. There it is. There's no denying it.'* Most companies now record telephone conversations. If you are disputing something with them, request a copy of that recording or at least a transcript of the conversation. They sometimes have a £10 charge for this but by asking for it, quite often they realise how adamant you are and will try to resolve the situation without going that far. It has worked for me time and again.

Summary

When dealing with the red tape of bureaucracy, follow the *Don't Get Done, Get Dom* guidelines:

- Don't give up too easily. Be persistent
- Remember there are three sides to every argument
- Don't be rude or aggressive
- Be firm, be adamant
- Show determination when the going gets tough
- When you meet a barrier, find a way around it
- Document every phone call, conversation, email and letter
- Build a paper trail of information
- Remember, the squeaky wheel gets the oil
- Make your voice heard!

CHAPTER TEN

How Do I Get My Money Back?

When you believe you are within your rights and entitled to a refund, persistence is the name of the game.

- **Know or learn your rights**
- **The law of distance selling**
- **The Sale of Goods Act and the Sale and Supply of Goods Act**
- **Refunds from retailers**
- **Holiday refunds**
- **Refunds for work on your home**

KNOW YOUR RIGHTS

People often assume they are entitled to their money back on any goods they buy, within a given time frame. Say, seven days. But that is not the case here in the UK. Did you know it can make a big difference where you were when you bought the item? Were you in the shop or showroom? Did you see what you bought first-hand, or did you place your order by telephone or over the internet? Those factors are important: they make a big difference to your rights.

Distance selling

Distance selling regulations give protection to consumers who shop by phone, mail order, via the internet or digital TV. The protection includes:

- The right to receive clear information about goods and services before deciding to buy
- Confirmation of this information in writing
- A cooling-off period of seven working days in which the consumer can withdraw from the contract
- Protection from credit card fraud

'A lot of people don't realise those regulations are in place in this country,' says Dom. 'Distance selling is classed as anything you've bought when you're not in front of the product or the salesperson. By law, from the day the item you've bought arrives, you can return it for any reason within seven days. Whether you don't like it, you don't like the colour, even if you've just changed your mind, it's irrelevant. You can send it back and you're entitled to a full refund. A lot of people aren't familiar with that.

'So technically you've got more rights if you buy something by phone, mail order, via the internet or digital TV than you have if you walk into a shop. When you buy something in a shop, if it proves to be faulty you're entitled to your money back. But if you take it back because you've decided you don't like it, you don't like the colour or it doesn't suit the settee, whatever, that's not seen as a justifiable reason for a refund. Just because you've changed your mind, it doesn't necessarily mean you're entitled to your money back.' A lot of shops will give you a refund or exchange as a gesture of goodwill anyway. Just don't expect it as the law.

A fact worth remembering if you want to maximise your rights.

'My brother benefited from that,' says Dom. 'He saw a settee he liked at the Ideal Home Exhibition. He didn't buy it there and then. He went home and checked the measurements, then ordered it over the telephone. When it arrived it wouldn't fit through the door and didn't suit his house at all. The retailer suggesting getting a tradesperson round to dismantle the settee and reassemble it once in the house. Because he'd ordered it by phone he was able to return it under the regulations of distance selling. So it's quite a powerful law and you are within your rights; there's no argument there.'

The Sale of Goods Act and the Sale and Supply of Goods Act

Dom has built up a good knowledge of consumer rights which is extremely helpful with his work on *Don't Get Done,*

Get Dom and he says there is another key area people don't always understand. When a manufacturer gives a warranty on a product, many of us believe our protection ends when that warranty runs out. But that is not the case.

'Funnily enough, manufacturers don't have to give you a warranty on any item they sell you. That is at their discretion. But I've phoned up and complained about items and the person has asked me how old the item is. When you say it's more than twelve months, they tell you it's out of warranty. Ninety-nine per cent of the time it's their ignorance and one per cent of the time it's them trying to play on your ignorance, because your legal rights are covered by the Sale of Goods Act which covers you for six years.

'There are two laws, actually, and it's a good idea to understand them both. Now the difference in them is, if you buy a boiler for your central-heating system you're covered under the Sale of Goods Act. But if you pay a plumber to supply and fit new central heating, that is covered under the Supply of Goods and Services Act. So what you've got there is his work and the product guaranteed. The way the law works, and this is a European law now, it covers you for six years.'

We have more protection than many of us realise.

'A lot of people think the length of the warranty is all you're entitled to. For the first six months you'll probably find the retailer, the supplier, will accept responsibility for any fault with the product and they'll revert back to the warranty that comes in the box with it. After six months – for the next five and a half years – it's up to you to prove that what's gone wrong is a manufacturer's fault and not a one-off.

'That's not actually the hardest thing to do with the advent of the internet and all the online information we now have access to. You can very easily search review sites and discussion forums and find people all over the world who have bought that product. If they've had the same problem, that's the evidence you need to go back and say, *Right, this TV is five years old and the tube's blown. It's an inherent problem, a manufacturer's problem, because here's a list of twenty people all around the world who've all had the same problem. It's down to you to sort it out.*

'You're covered for six years in total. If you have a problem, go to your retailer first and if the shop is no longer in business, or won't help you, then go to the manufacturer second. Speak to them and explain your problem. Tell them how much you've been quoted for the repair and that you expect them to pay their percentage of it. That amount is the only grey area because they can't put it in black and white for the simple reason they can't list every problem on every product, so you negotiate.

'When it comes to agreeing a figure, you've got to use your common sense. If a product goes wrong just after the warranty has run out then I would expect them to pay 80, 90 per cent of the repair cost. That's what I'd ask for. But if the product is five, five and a half years old, then I'd be quite happy to accept 50–50, or perhaps even 70–30 in their favour. You've got to be reasonable.'

Refunds from retailers

As Dom has pointed out, you need to know you are in the right when you go into a shop asking for a refund. If you are sure of your facts, show them you feel confident.

'You've got to be courteous and polite,' says Dom. 'I'm a great believer in that. But you must be firm too, because some people see politeness as weakness. You've got to make them realise you are a polite person with a problem that has to be sorted out. If they see you looking down at your hands and feet, showing signs of being shy and nervous and a bit uncomfortable, they'll fob you off and get you out the door quicker than you can sneeze. So stay polite, but keep looking them in the eyes. It's down to psychology again, make eye-to-eye contact with them at all times. Don't be fobbed off. Be determined, be firm and don't start losing your rag if things aren't going your way.

'If you're not getting on with the person you're speaking to, or that person is unable to resolve your issues, try to speak to someone in a higher position who might take you more seriously. If the person you're talking to isn't helpful, you need to move on. Just be honest and say, *Obviously you're not the person who can sort out this problem, you're not in a position to do that, so who's in charge here?*

'Occasionally, the person you're speaking to might say, *I'm in charge here, take it or leave it*. At that point, if you can't get the problem sorted out at that particular branch, then you start going above them. But try and think about the best psychology to use in the situation. Rather than getting angry and saying you're going to write to head office and complain, it's better to do it in a different way.

'Explain if they can't rectify the situation now, then you'd like them to give you the contact details for their head office, preferably the CEO's name and number if they are able to issue that. Say to them, *That's on the understanding you can't help me now. If you sort it out today, fine, I don't need to speak to them*. Now that's a very good way of saying, *Listen, I'm not giving up, I will take this further, but I'm going to give you another crack at trying to resolve this situation*.

'Whatever the problem is it's always good psychology to give them a way out. They have tried to fob you off and get rid of you. Everybody does when you've got a problem; they don't want to deal with you. But if you are firm and determined, they'll realise you're not going to let it drop. They can see you'll be on the phone to head office moaning and groaning. The salesperson will think, *I just don't need this*. Give them a chance, in your polite, firm way, to sort things out. Don't close the door, leave a way forward open.

'By not backing them into a corner, you give them the chance to come back and say, *You can have head office's details, but I'll tell you what I can do, right? I can't give you a full refund, but I can let you have this one at sale price and I'll throw in some DVDs or whatever. Are you happy with that?* They'll quite often come back with an offer like that. Listen to what they have to say and judge each situation on its merits. Hopefully you'll find the common ground and reach a settlement that suits both sides.

'It's worth remembering that salespeople quite often have a justifiable reason for not giving you a refund, a replacement, or whatever. It's not always the case that you're right, and they're wrong. If you return something you've bought at a shop and it's not faulty, getting your money back is at their discretion. Some shops have a notice up saying we do not give refunds, we only give credit notes. Okay. They are within their rights to do that. The only time they've got to give you a refund is if something's faulty.'

How long do you have to take a faulty item back after you've bought it?

'Twenty-eight days. Say you've bought a shirt and when you try it on at home you find there's a tear in it, or some of the stitching is coming away, you can take it back and say you want the shop to replace it or refund your money. If it's faulty there's no argument there. If the shop does refuse to give you your money back, you can go to the Small Claims Court to get the matter resolved. But if you're in the right, that really shouldn't be necessary.'

Holiday refunds

Dom has been involved with sorting out a long list of holiday disputes on the series. These are cases where people have had such a disappointing trip they feel totally justified in asking for their money back. Making that refund happen can be difficult and time consuming. How can we ensure we are in the best position to get that refund if a dream holiday turns into a nightmare? In Dom's opinion, it starts on the day you book.

'If you book a package holiday and you then have a problem when you are away, you can go back to the company who supplied the holiday. If you book everything separately you'll be told to complain to the hotel or the airline independently.'

Chasing disputes with hotels abroad, once you are back in the UK, can be extremely difficult. There are various factors to overcome, including the cost of phone calls, possible language barriers and the sheer distance between you and the people you are complaining to. It can be a tiring and complicated process.

'Legally you have more power with a package holiday,' says Dom. 'So unless something is considerably cheaper, there's no point in booking it any other way. Book a package; I always do when I have that option.'

How you pay for your holiday is important too.

'Booking with a credit card can give you extra protection,' Dom explains. 'If you've had a holiday nightmare or the flights have let you down or something's been stolen and your room's been burgled, you might well find you're covered under the insurance you get with your credit card. It gives you another avenue of complaint. Whereas if you paid by cash, debit card or cheque, you've got no protection there at all. You may get charged an extra one or two per cent when you book with a credit card, but it's worth doing because of the extra cover you get.'

If things start to go wrong once you are on holiday, what evidence should you gather to strengthen your case for a refund when you get home?

'One obvious piece of advice is to take photos, videos, and record whatever you can to document the situation over there. Then when you get home attach a photo to your letter of complaint. If possible, print the photo into your letter or just staple or glue it on there. Make your complaint letter different to everyone else's. Make it clear you have a genuine grievance. Get a good close-up, a good-quality picture that clearly shows the reason you had such a terrible holiday.

'When you write your letter, don't waffle on about things that aren't relevant to your complaint. Stick to the key points. Tell them what went wrong: you're unhappy and you expect them to do something about it. Just put that into short, polite, firm words. Don't take a page to say what you can put in a paragraph, because people will just skim over it.'

What else can you do to strengthen your case for compensation while you are away?

'What you should do is exchange details, phone numbers and email addresses, with other holidaymakers who are having the same problems on the holiday. Form a group. A lot of people do that, liaise when they get back and keep each other informed of what's happening, because then might is right, isn't it? The more people that complain about the same problem, the more effect you're going to have when you get home.

'I would say first of all go back to the company or travel agent you booked your package holiday with. Try and get resolution, some sort of agreement both sides are happy with. If they offer compensation or vouchers or whatever, you don't necessarily have to accept that. You can negotiate and ask for more or you can decide to take things further and go for a full refund if you feel that is what you deserve.

'Travel Watch (www.holidaytravelwatch.net) are there as a governing body for the travel industry, and they will advise you. They're not worried about who they're upsetting because none of the groups they deal with, i.e. the travel companies and airlines, etc., are paying members. There are a lot of different organisations out there who can help. Do your research and make sure you get independent advice, that's crucial.

'If you can't settle the dispute amicably, then you can always go to the Small Claims Court for anything up to £5,000. That is the maximum they can award. If you want to make a larger claim you can go to County Court, but you will normally end up getting legal representation, as will the people defending the case, so it's a lot more costly.

'The Small Claims Court is really easy to deal with. It's not like going to a court where you're there with a judge and a jury and you have people taking minutes of the hearing, etc. At a Small Claims Court you go into a room and there will be one judge. It's meant to be very informal. You state your case, the other side states theirs. The judge usually gives a decision immediately after the trial but in rare cases both parties are informed of the outcome of the trial a few days later by mail.

'I think the Small Claims Court is a very good way of sorting out disputes between people. What I would say if you go down that line, is never be ignorant of the law because the judge will not be happy with that at all. They do not like ignorance of the law, so make sure you research your case. Again, don't waffle, give your points, state your facts, outline what you're trying to claim be calm at all times and the judge will give his or her decision.

'But going to court should be your last option. Whatever the dispute, a nightmare holiday or anything else, try and resolve things before they get to that stage if you possibly can.' You can find out information about the Small Claims Court at www.hmcourts-service.gov.uk

Refunds for work on your home

Building work, plumbing, central-heating systems, conservatories and double glazing. Dom has dealt with all sorts of problems around the home, where people want their money back for shoddy work. But when setting out to resolve a dispute, Dom comes back to his earlier advice:

- Make sure you know your rights
- There are three sides to every story: yours, theirs and the truth
- Keep an open mind

'For starters, you might not be entitled to your money back,' he says. 'If a builder has made a poor job of the plastering, it doesn't necessarily mean you can get a full refund, because the brickwork he's done might be brilliant. So there needs to be an element of percentage there. But if what he's done has been really bad right from the start, and everything needs pulling down and redoing, then you need to get all your money back.

'Unfortunately, a lot of tradespeople are quite often small outfits and they will put up quite an argument in their defence and do everything they can not to give you your money back. The first thing I would do is get an independent survey done on the work. If it's poor, you have to get that documented. Get it in writing, because if the dispute does end up going to court, you will need to have an independent opinion. The fact that you think the work that has been done is bad and the builder doesn't agree is not an argument in court. As long as you've got evidence and you've backed it up, you've done the right thing.

'Then you should speak to people like Citizens Advice Bureau (www.citizensadvice.org.uk), Consumer Direct (www.consumerdirect.gov.uk) or Which? Legal Service (www.whichlegalservice.co.uk). Get their advice because the chances are you don't know the legal process. Find out what those people recommend. If you don't want the original builder to come back and rectify the work then you have to give them the option to pay. Say, *I want to get somebody independent to you to do the repair. I've got a quote here.* Send them a photocopy of that. State your case, *We've been told the work you carried out is not up to standard, it's been condemned,* whatever the case is. *I want somebody else to do the work, here is the amount of money it will cost. I expect you to pay this. Please send me a cheque . . .*

'Give the builder or tradesperson an option to rectify the situation before it gets nasty. Quite often they might well say, *Okay, I had a go at doing the electrics, shouldn't really have done that, couldn't do it, so here's a cheque for whatever it is*. They will sort it out. So give them a chance to put the job right or an option to pay for another tradesperson to come around and put it right. Depending on the case, you might expect them to pay in full or a percentage of the costs. That's the courteous way to do it. If things deteriorate from there then unfortunately you'll probably end up taking them to court.'

One good way of avoiding poor workmanship is to enlist the help of organisations like Trustmark (www.trustmark.org.uk) who will help you to find reliable, trustworthy tradesmen to make improvements and repairs inside and outside your home. The scheme is supported by Government, the building industry and consumer protection groups. Firms who work with Trustmark are able to offer customers an insurance-backed warranty, which can prove to be a real asset should any dispute arise. There are numerous web sites that have local tradespeople who have been recommended by customers for the quality of their work. One such site is www.ratedpeople.com

Dom says there are other areas you should check too.

'You might possibly have legal protection with the building and contents insurance on your property, where if something goes wrong you can ask your household insurance company to intervene and take up the case.'

In disputes of this kind, the road to resolution is often a rocky one.

'Unfortunately disputes with tradespeople often go to court,' says Dom. 'It will regularly get quite messy, but you've got to try and get out of it as best you can. Be firm, be persistent, don't be rude. Don't expect a full refund unless you're actually entitled to one. Quite often there might be an element of wear and tear, so evaluate every situation. Work out what you want and ask yourself if you are being fair in what you are requesting. Don't expect a five thousand pound compensation cheque for something that cost you three hundred pounds to buy, unless there's a reason for that: you've been injured, you've been hurt, or there's been damage caused.

'Always document every single complaint from start to finish: who you spoke to, the days, the times that you called, what number you called from. Never lose your temper and always stay within the law. Don't start making threats because before you know it, you could actually be charged with making aggressive phone calls or harassment. Never, ever be rude, sexist, racist or anything else, no matter how you feel about the person you're dealing with.

'Be firm, be polite. Know your rights. Don't be ignorant. Don't demand what you're not entitled to, and if you're seeking compensation be realistic.'

Summary

When chasing the refund you deserve, follow the *Don't Get Done, Get Dom* guidelines:

- Know and understand your rights
- Did you buy in person or by phone or internet? It makes a difference
- Give people a chance to resolve your complaint
- Don't close the door on negotiations: leave a way forward
- If you have a holiday nightmare, document the situation at the location
- Form an action group with other dissatisfied holiday-makers
- If you have problems with work at your home, get an independent survey
- Try to settle disputes amicably if at all possible
- Be fair in what you ask for
- Make going to court a final resort
- Document your complaint from start to finish

CHAPTER ELEVEN

Consumer Action

In this strand of the TV series, Dom tackles social injustice and red tape on behalf of viewers. Here he gives his expert advice on a range of topics exclusively for you.

- The car trade
- Local councils
- The Tax Office
- Credit cards
- Your credit rating
- The internet
- Utility bills

One of the most remarkable features of the first three series of *Don't Get Done, Get Dom* has been the wide variety of subjects covered in the programme's Consumer Advice slots. Dom worked on all 60 shows and shared a great deal of knowledge from the stories he covered.

In this chapter he shares his take on some of the topics the series covered. Before making his name on TV, Dom was a very successful car salesperson, so it makes sense to start with his advice and thoughts on a world he knows very well indeed.

The car trade

'When you buy a car, it can sometimes be beneficial to use car finance,' says Dom 'but only if the interest rates are competitive. 'That can help if you have problems with the vehicle, because your legal agreement is with the car finance company. You make your payments to them and they still own the car. The day you make your very last payment, is the day you become the legal owner. Until then the finance company is supplying you with the car on a 'hire' basis.

'If something goes wrong with it, the first thing you should do is go back to the supplier. That's good common sense; the courteous thing to do. Tell the garage what the problem is, but bear in mind it might not be something that's covered under warranty. Wear and tear items aren't covered, for example. But if the fault is mechanical and you think you're covered, go back to the supplier and say, *This is what's gone wrong and you're responsible*. If they try to fob you off, you can then turn to the car finance company. A lot of people don't realise you're covered that way.

'Buying on car finance gives you another string to your bow. If the garage doesn't sort your problem out you can go to the finance company and say, *Right, you supplied me with this car, it's faulty, I think you should pay for it.* Now that's the angle to take. They may argue that the car's done thirty thousand miles, it's five years old or whatever. But you can then ask how big a percentage of the cost of repair they will pay. It might be a 50–50 contribution, which is still very useful when dealing with an expensive repair.

'Use that extra string to your bow. Let me reiterate this. It's got to be higher purchase finance on the car, not a bank loan, a personal loan, personal savings or remortgage of your house for money for a car. Those things are irrelevant, whereas car finance is secured on the car.

'If a car you've bought from a garage develops a mechanical fault that is not down to regular wear and tear, there are three things you can do:

1. Go back to the supplier you bought it from and give them the chance to put the fault right.
2. Complain to the finance company you are buying the car from.
3. Worst-case scenario, you can also contact the manufacturers. Manufacturers should be fairly understanding if the car's not too old, say a couple of years with low mileage. They will tend to start putting up more barriers the older the car gets, but you still have a case with them.

Dom has sorted out a number of disputes with garages on the series. But it's important to remember that many other garages all over the country give good and professional service and honour their commitments to customers. When you buy a car from a reputable garage, you should feel you can take it back if things go wrong. But if you choose to buy privately, your rights are greatly diminished.

'When you buy a car from a garage nowadays you'll get a warranty with it,' Dom explains. 'You'll save money if you buy it privately, but you've got virtually no legal comeback at all, so you'll have to be extra cautious. You'll need to check the car's not on finance and that it hasn't been involved in any major accidents. Check that the person selling the car does actually own it and that all the details they've given you are correct. I'd say, if you don't have a good knowledge of cars, pay somebody to look over it for you. You can use people like the AA (www.theaa.com) or the RAC (http://breakdown.rac.co.uk).

'Motoring organisations like that have different levels of checks, but they will normally be insurance-backed, so if there's a problem within six months, for example if you find out the car is two halves welded together five months down the line, you'll be covered by their insurance.

'The alternative is to ask a local mechanic. There are lots of mechanics out there who would charge you £25 or £50 to come round and give the car the once-over in their lunch hour. How do you find a mechanic you can trust? I'd go to a reputable garage and find someone who's working there who looks like they know what they're talking about. If you get an experienced mechanic to look at the quality and the condition of a car, chances are they'll know their products. That's their job. That's what I'd do if I was buying privately. I'd also do that if I was buying from a second-hand garage, not a big main agent. I'd get a mechanic to have a look; it's definitely advisable.'

Local councils

When taking a problem to your local council, it often involves the familiar scenario of working your way up the chain until you get the issue resolved. Dom's usual advice of noting every telephone call, email, message and conversation applies here too.

'Always try and resolve the problem locally first,' says Dom. 'Speak to someone in the relevant council department first. Then, if you need to, move on to the department manager. People I've helped with local issues on the show have often got to that stage, but their problem still hasn't been dealt with. When that's the case, I've found the best person to speak to next is the council leader. They are very good at listening to problems and then delegating. The second that happens I find councils become easier to resolve problems with.

'The only downside with councils is there's a lot of bureaucracy which means they have to go through certain Board of Governors meetings and other bureaucratic hurdles. Then they have to get their own solicitors to look at things or their own surveyors to sort problems out. It's a slow process, but if you speak to the right person you'll get the chain moving. Only use the council leader as a last resort. There's no point in going straight to them because quite often you can sort out the problem in the department itself.'

But what do you do if you work your way up the chain all the way to the council leader and your problem is still not resolved?

'What about going to the MP?' asks Dom. 'There's always someone higher. Try your town mayor. Go to your MP. Be that squeaky wheel, be that monkey, and they will think: *Oh my God, this person just won't get off my back. He's gone from David Smith in the office, to Dave's manager, then he went to the superior in charge. He spoke to the council leader, now he's gone to the opposition party and you know they'll jump on anyone to get a story. And guess what? He's only written to the mayor, as well. Just get this person off my case!*

'There's always somebody else you can go to. Don't let that wall stop you: it's just an obstacle you've got to get over.'

The Tax Office

Next Dom gives some advice on what to do if you've got problems with the Tax Office, like some of the people he has helped on *Don't Get Done, Get Dom*.

'The big problem you have with tax is it's so complex,' he says. 'Most people don't understand it and I'm no expert myself. Even accountants can learn new things every day. What I'd say, in general terms, is that the Tax Office is not this big, dark monster that hides down in the dungeon. Modern-day tax officials will talk to you. You can go in and have a chat, meet them, or have a discussion on the phone. They are there to help you out. They're very, very reasonable people to deal with.

'Don't be scared when dealing with the Tax Office. Most people are. Certainly in the past people didn't know how to contact them, how to speak to them, and thought everything was complicated. That's changed, they are more approachable now. You don't necessarily have to get independent advice, you can phone them up and say, *This is what I don't understand, what's wrong, is it you or is it me?*'

But if you are still confused about the tax issue affecting you, even after talking to the Tax Office, then it really is time to call in some professional help.

'You don't have to be in business to have an accountant,'

says Dom. 'They are often quite happy to deal with one-off issues. A lot of people don't realise that. Somebody I spoke to recently had an issue with something that happened many, many years ago. The Tax Office had written to them and they were a bit worried about things, they didn't know what to do. I said they should go and speak to an accountant and they did. The accountant took their case on board, addressed it and resolved it in no time at all.

'Quite often the Tax Office like it when an accountant deals with issues. They find it easier to deal with someone who knows the ground rules. It means they haven't got to explain everything in black and white. Another thing to bear in mind is that being represented by a tax expert takes all the weight of pressure off you.

'Don't try and avoid tax. We all have to pay it. It's what keeps the country running. But the Tax Office can make mistakes, and you can negotiate with them on certain things. You can say, *Well, actually I disagree with you on this*, and they will allow you to put your point across. Don't be scared of them. They are not a big monster. They're a necessity. We all want to pay what we have to pay and that's all, so if you have a problem, speak to them and if you're still not sure, seek independent advice.'

Credit cards

'I'm a great believer in using credit cards,' says Dom. 'Obviously not if you can't afford to pay the money back. It's a bad way to get in debt. The best way to use credit cards, if you possibly can, is to pay off your bill in full each month. I do that. I've got a direct debit set up so I can't forget to make a payment. It happens automatically. Credit card companies will never earn a penny in interest out of me.'

Setting up a direct debit at your bank to deal with your monthly credit card bill is easy and straightforward. But, once again, it's something many of us have never thought of doing.

'You tell your bank what you want to pay,' Dom explains. 'It might be the minimum payment stated on the bill, a pre-set amount which you choose or you can have the full amount paid each month. Mine is paid in full every single month, so I use a credit card for virtually everything. I don't pay any interest because I never miss a payment. If for any reason the payment is late, it's the bank's fault. It's a very, very good way to buy things . . . and because I chose a cash back card supplier I get cash back on what I spend.'

Your credit rating

'Everyone in this country, literally from the age of being able to get credit, will have a credit rating. There are three companies that keep our ratings. They're called Callcredit (www.callcredit.co.uk), Experian (www.experian.co.uk) and Equifax (www.equifax.co.uk). Legally you can check up on your own credit rating. It costs you about two pounds per application, so a maximum of six pounds to check the information that all three companies have on you.

'You could have information stored against you which is detrimental to you getting credit in future. What the sites allow you to do is write to justify and explain why there's a bad mark against you. It's normally up to two hundred words. There are circumstances where we all have glitches in our credit history. It could be because you're going through a split or divorce. Maybe there's been a death in the family. It might be because you've lost a job, perhaps through illness or redundancy. It could be due to lots of different reasons and credit card companies – not just credit card companies, any other credit companies – are aware of these situations. They will understand if you've had problems.

'The important thing is not to put your head under the pillow and think things will go away. If there is a problem there, you need to rectify it. If you're buying on credit and the company looks at your credit rating and reads the information you have supplied to the website, explaining the reason for that period of time when you didn't make payments, then they will know you've had a glitch and, fine, they'll understand that. Also, they will really like the fact that you've actually had the decency to respond to the information on the site and explain the mitigating circumstances. That shows that you are probably a good person to lend money to. So don't run away: face the problem and deal with it as honestly as you can.'

You may find the details of your credit report vary from site to site. What do you do if your report contains information that is simply not true?

'If there's something on one of the sites that shouldn't be there, don't contact them direct. You need to write to the company that put the information on the site and tell them they've got the wrong person, wrong address or wrong information. Then it's up to that company to tell the credit company the information in your credit rating is wrong and have it removed. You must check to make sure that happens.'

If your credit rating is genuinely poor, that is something you will have to live with.

'Credit problems won't disappear,' says Dom. 'If you've got County Court Judgments (CCJ's), if you've got a slow payment profile, or a non-payment profile, it will go on your credit rating. The worse your history, the more there is going to be on there. The more that's on there, the worse it's going to be for you.

'Every time you apply to get credit, a search will go against your name. You must be careful not to apply at loads of different places at the same time and think it's clever and you'll take whichever one suits you. All those applications will be registered as searches, and when a card company, or any company that's about to give you credit, looks and sees that suddenly there have been eight searches against your name in the past week, that is a big, big no for them. You won't get your credit. Always apply with just one, or maximum two, companies. Basically, do your homework. Find out who you want to get that particular credit from and then apply. Don't just go willy-nilly and start applying for it with loads of credit companies, because it will go against you.'

The internet

Dom thoroughly enjoys going out for a little retail therapy, but he often buys products on the internet too.

'When you buy on the internet you're covered by the Distance Selling Regulations I talked about earlier. You have seven days to return the goods for any reason whatsoever. So the internet is a clever way to buy things, but you do need to be careful. Never, ever give any payment details, credit card details or any other finance details, unless it's a site you have gone to directly. If an email comes through and it's asking you to click on a linked page and give your credit details, don't ever do it. That is called phishing and it's the criminally fraudulent process of attempting to acquire sensitive information. Avoid it. The only time to give information is when you have gone to a site, you know what the site is and you know what you're buying. You are expecting to use your credit card to pay, so that's fair enough.'

Once again, very good advice. On a lighter note, Dom often takes the haggling skills he shows on *Don't Get Done, Get Dom* a stage further and uses them on the internet!

'People don't realise you can do that,' he says. 'They believe the price you see on the screen is what you've got to pay. I'm totally the opposite, I haggle on everything. Whether it's eBay, retail stores, shops, whatever. Nearly all the websites give Contact Us information; it might be a phone number and address or just an email. Whatever format it comes in, contact the shop. It's best to ring them up, but send an email if that's the only way of contacting them and say, *Look, I've seen such and such, these four wall lights, and you're advertising them for that. If you can do something on the price, I will order them today.* I do it and I can tell you it's probably 99 per cent successful. You *will* get the price down.

'Just because you find a company on the internet, it doesn't mean they're faceless. Get in contact and haggle: I get everything down in price on the internet, no matter what it is.'

Dom's haggling skills are legendary, but he still enjoys the fun and satisfaction that comes from a deal well done.

'I bought four lights last week, in fact they're due to be delivered any day now. I saw them in a shop and they were £115 each. Really nice lights, so I had a haggle with the salesperson who dropped them down to £82. I said, I wasn't happy with the price and gave him an opportunity to better it and he didn't, so fine, I left on good terms so I could always go back. All the things I say to people on the programme.

'When I got home I went on the Internet and I found the same lights for £60 each. I wanted four of them, so we're talking £240. I found the contact details of the guy who was selling them and phoned him up. He owns a shop, his name was Luke, and I got talking to him. I didn't give my name. I've never, ever used the influence of television to get a better deal, or anything else. I never tell people who I am when I'm talking on the phone. Some people recognise my voice immediately, but not in this case. I just said I'd seen the lights on his site, I liked them but I didn't want to spend £240. Eventually he dropped them down to £192, which was a massive saving of £268 from the first shop I had visited and, it meant I'd saved £48 for the price of a phone call.

'So if people tell you it's impossible to haggle on the internet, don't believe them. Try it for yourself, you'll find it works!'

Utility bills

And finally, some advice on those household bills we all have to pay. Dom has resolved various problems with utility companies on the show.

'One of the things I found out through doing research for the programme was that rather than dealing with the actual utility company themselves, there was a regulator who you could go to. The one I used was called Energywatch, an independent organisation representing the interests of gas and electricity consumers in Great Britain.'

Energywatch has now merged with Postwatch and the Welsh, Scottish and National Consumer Councils to form Consumer Focus (http://www.consumerfocus.org.uk).

'Energywatch, as they were then, advised me of things I wasn't aware of. I'm not an encyclopedia of knowledge. I don't know everything. I'm fairly switched on with lots of things, but by speaking to this regulator I found out some very useful information. They told me that where pre-payment meters are concerned, if somebody makes a complaint there's a law out there that says the utility companies have to respond within a certain amount of time. With the case I was working on it was within three hours. If the utility company didn't respond and rectify the situation within three hours, you were automatically entitled to £20 compensation. And that was for each and every three hours they didn't turn up.

'So, by doing my homework and not just going in like a bull in a china shop demanding everything from the utility company, I made that discovery. Having that information was quite powerful, because then I knew that if you complain and they don't turn up, it actually works in your favour. Great!'

Dom's advice is to avoid pre-payment gas and electricity meters if you possibly can.

'Personally I would say to anybody, don't have those meters full stop. You pay a more expensive charge rate on them. They are normally used by people who often can't afford the big bills when they come in. It's a way of spreading the cost. But if you're paying more, it's a catch-22. They're very, very expensive.'

What about ordinary utility bills? If you are not happy with what you are being charged, what's your best course of action there?

'The first thing I'd say is you need to bear in mind that these meters are normally accurate, so the chances there is something wrong are very slim. What people normally have complaints with, where you might have some sort of argument, is where you're paying too much on your direct debit or you don't think your bill arrived. The chances are you're not actually right. It's very rare for these things to be wrong, but phone up and speak to the energy company you deal with. Once again, get names, get numbers. If you need more help speak to the regulators or the watchdogs, tell them what your problem is, and see if you have a justifiable argument.

'Quite often people have problems because they can't afford to pay a bill or they're misusing energy or overusing it. Quite often energy companies will have a department which will help people who are struggling. Talk to them. The company might be doing nothing wrong. It could just be that you're being foolish. If so, you need advice: you're not on the best plan, you're not budgeting correctly or paying in the best way.

'So again, it comes back to not being aggressive in the way you deal with the problem. Speak to the company, find out what your options are. If you still think something's wrong, try and get them to resolve it. If they won't, then speak to the regulators or the watchdogs or the Ombudsman. There are always people out there who will advise you. If you don't know where to find them, speak to the people who do: Citizens Advice Bureau (www.citizensadvice.org.uk) or Consumer Direct (www.consumerdirect.gov.uk) or National Debtline (www.nationaldebtline.co.uk).

'Organisations like that will advise at no cost. They are there to help you.'

CHAPTER TWELVE

•

Reflections

Dom's closing thoughts on this book and what he hopes it will achieve.

A REAL BUZZ

Over a million people regularly watched the 60 programmes in the first three series of *Don't Get Done, Get Dom*. Now BBC One have commissioned Flame TV, the production company, to produce a new season of ten programmes to be screened in 2010. Why is the series so successful? Well, as this book has shown, it is crammed full of excellent advice.

When Dominic Littlewood reflects on all the assignments he has covered and the thousands of miles he has travelled to meet and help the people who have appeared on the show, he feels all the hard work has been worthwhile. He knows viewers love the programme and that means a lot to him.

Haggling

'I get a real buzz when people come up and say they enjoy what I do and find it helpful. Some tell me how they have used my haggling tips to save money. Sometimes it's just a small amount; maybe some cushions thrown in with a settee. But it's a start: they feel good about what they've achieved and I love that. Teaching people how to haggle is fun. I like taking them out of their comfort zones and showing that what they've been terrified of doing is actually quite an enjoyable experience.

'I hope the people who read this book will use the guidelines I've given to try haggling for themselves. Just have a go and you'll find the fun and banter become addictive. You'll start enjoying shopping more, especially when you get some discount, free extras or both. You'll get better and better and better at it until you get to a stage when you'll walk in and get a discount without even blinking an eyelid, because you know you can. I want people to lose that British reserve and this book will help them to do that.'

Consumer advice

Sorting out people's problems is a more serious issue.

'The people I help have often had the problem they've called me in to deal with for six months or more. They've tried to sort it out for themselves but the lack of progress has left them angry and frustrated. The situation has been driving them up the wall. So it's very satisfying when I get a result and can go and tell them the good news. I've sorted it out, here's some compensation. You've got this, you've got that. When I look at their faces and see them light up, it's a great feeling and a weight off my shoulders.'

Dom gets really involved with some of the more extreme cases he deals with in the series.

'I don't like it when people get shafted by villains. When they pick on everyday people . . . no, I'm not having it. Someone messes with them, someone rips them off, and I'm going to be their worst enemy. Dealing with situations like that can be tough. I can't say I love it. It's often aggravation after aggravation. But I'm like a bulldog, when I get my teeth into a problem I won't let go. If a case I was tackling for people was not resolved by the end of the series, I'd keep fighting using my own time and money until it was sorted out. The cases that offer a real challenge are the ones I absolutely thrive on. I'm very stubborn, I don't give up.'

Stand up for your rights

Dom hopes this book will empower readers to stand up for their rights.

'Anyone can do it. People might think I only get results because I'm on the telly, but that's not true. I've been doing this since I first learnt how to read, write and speak. If I wasn't happy with things, I sorted them out. I am a man who stands up for his rights. We can all do it. We mustn't be scared to stand up to the big boys when we know we are in the right. If there's one message I'd like to get across it's that.'

Positive messages

Whether you are haggling for a discount in the high street or on the internet, chasing your money back in a dispute or cutting through red tape in a bureaucratic wrangle, let this book be your guide to facing life with determination, persistence and, when appropriate, a cheeky smile and sense of fun. Make the positive messages in these pages part of your life in future.

Don't Get Done, Get Dom!

PART 3

•

The Hit List

CHAPTER THIRTEEN

Who Should I Turn To?

A list of useful contacts and organisations offering expert consumer advice.

Consumer Direct

Consumer Direct is the government-funded telephone and online service offering information and advice on consumer issues. Consumer Direct is funded by the Office of Fair Trading and delivered in partnership with Local Authority Trading Standards Services. They provide clear, practical, impartial advice to help you sort out problems and disagreements you may be having with suppliers of goods or services.
08454 04 05 06
http://www.consumerdirect.gov.uk/

Trading Standards Institute

To find the number for your nearest Trading Standards office as well as to see useful consumer information, see
http://www.tradingstandards.gov.uk/advice/consumer-advice.cfm

Sale of Goods Act:
1979 – http://www.johnantell.co.uk/SOGA1979.htm
1994 – http://www.opsi.gov.uk/acts/acts1994/Ukpga_19940035_en_1.htm

Financial Ombudsman

They deal with complaints about: banking services, credit cards issued by banks and building societies, endowment policies, financial and investment advice, health and private medical insurance, income and loan protection cover, household and buildings insurance, investment and portfolio management, life assurance, mortgages, motor insurance, National Savings & Investments (NS&I), personal pension

plans, savings plans and accounts, stocks and shares, travel insurance, unit trusts and income bonds.
http://www.financial-ombudsman.org.uk/

Local Government Ombudsman

The Local Government Ombudsman investigates complaints about councils and certain other bodies. They investigate complaints about most council matters including housing, planning, education and social services.
http://www.lgo.org.uk/

Consumer Focus

Consumer Focus was created through the merger of three consumer organisations – Energywatch, Postwatch and the National Consumer Council (including the Welsh and Scottish Consumer Councils).
www.consumerfocus.org.uk/

Energywatch
http://www.energywatch.org.uk/
08459 06 07 08

Post Watch
http://www.postwatch.co.uk/

National Consumer Council
http://www.ncc.org.uk/

Citizens Advice Bureau (CAB)

Help on a variety of problems. To find your local CAB look at their website www.citizensadvice.org.uk

Advertising Standards Authority (ASA)

The ASA investigates complaints about advertisements, sales promotions and direct marketing.
www.asa.org.uk

Law Centres

Provide free advice by solicitors and specialist caseworkers in areas such as employment, immigration, welfare benefits, housing and discrimination. To find your local office, look at their website www.lawcentres.org.uk

Ombudsman

The British and Irish Ombudsman Association publishes a directory of ombudsman schemes and complaint-handling bodies in the UK and Ireland.
www.bioa.org.uk

Arbitration

- **Chartered Institute of Arbitrators**
  Details of their consumer scheme are at their website.
  www.arbitrators.org

- **Scottish Council for Arbitration**
  Details of their schemes can be found at their website.
  www.scottish-arbitrators.org

Cars

- **The National Conciliation Service**
  Deals with complaints about used cars, repairs and servicing in England, Wales and Northern Ireland.
  www.rmif.co.uk

- **Customer Complaints Service, Scottish Motor Trade Association**
  Deals with complaints about used cars, repairs and servicing in Scotland.
  www.smta.co.uk

- **The Society of Motor Manufacturers and Traders**
  Complaints about cars still under a manufacturer's warranty.
  www.smmt.co.uk

- **Vehicle Builders and Repairers Association**
  Administers a code of practice for its car body repairers which has been approved by the OFT, and has complaint-handling procedures including access to an independent redress mechanism.
  www.vbra.co.uk

- **British Vehicle Rental and Leasing Association**
  Deals with complaints about car rental and lease in the UK.
  www.bvrla.co.uk

Credit and debt

- **Federation of Information and Advice Centres (FIAC)**
  Contact independent advice agencies through the FIAC.
  www.adviceuk.org.uk

- **National Debtline**
  Telephone helpline for people with debt problems.
  www.nationaldebtline.co.uk

- **Consumer Credit Counselling Service**
  Provides free confidential service to help achieve realistic solutions to debt problems, avoid bankruptcy and learn to handle money.
  www.cccs.co.uk 0845 40 40 50 6

- **Financial Services Compensation Scheme**
  Acts as a final safety net for consumers who have claims against authorised financial firms who are unable to pay them because, for example, they have gone out of business. It covers deposits, insurance and investments.
  www.fscs.org.uk

- **Financial Ombudsman Scheme**
  Provides consumers with free independent advice for resolving disputes with financial firms.
  www.financial-ombudsman.org.uk

Direct selling

- **Direct Selling Association**
  Administers a code of practice for its direct selling members, such as Avon, Betterware, etc., which has been approved by the OFT and has complaint-handling procedures, including access to an independent redress mechanism.
  http://dsa.org.uk/

Electrical goods

- **Radio Electrical and Television Retailers' Association Ltd**
  Find out whether a retailer is a member at their website.
  www.retra.co.uk

- **Association of Manufacturers of Domestic Electrical Appliances**
  Find out whether a retailer is a member at their website.
  www.amdea.org.uk

- **Domestic Appliance Service Association**
  Find out whether a retailer is a member at their website.
  www.dasa.org.uk

Estate agents

- **Ombudsman for Estate Agents Scheme**
  Administers a code of practice for its members engaged in residential sales which has been approved by the OFT and has complaint-handling procedures.
  www.oea.co.uk

Furniture and home-furnishing

- **The Furniture Ombudsman**
  The independent standards body for furniture (including floor coverings, kitchens and bathrooms). The Furniture Ombudsman provides a dispute resolution service and can perform on-site inspections of products.
  http://www.fira.co.uk/services/furniture Ombudsman.html

- **The Carpet Foundation**
  The Carpet Foundation administers a code of practice for its carpet retailers which has been approved by the OFT and has complaint-handling procedures.
  www.carpetfoundation.com

Holidays

- **Air Travel Organiser's Licence (ATOL)**
  ATOL protects the public from losing money or being stranded abroad because of the failure of air travel firms.
  www.atol.org.uk

- **Association of British Travel Agents (ABTA)**
  Offers advice on travel-related subjects and can verify whether a travel agent or tour operator is a member of ABTA.
  www.abta.com

- **Air Transport Users Council**
  Advise air travellers on their rights.
  www.auc.org.uk

- **Civil Aviation Authority – Consumer Protection Group**
  http://www.caa.co.uk/default.aspx?catid=6

- **Customs and Excise**
  Offers advice on customs and excise.
  www.hmrc.gov.uk

- **Holiday Travel Watch**
  Consumer group.
  http://www.holidaytravelwatch.net/Default.aspx

- **HolidayWatchdog.com**
  Consumer group.
  http://www.holidaywatchdog.com/

Legal services

- **Competition Pro Bono Scheme**
  The Competition Pro Bono Scheme offers some free legal advice to individuals and businesses who believe that their rights under competition law have been infringed or who are concerned that they may be infringing.
  www.probonogroup.org.uk/competition

- **Legal Services Ombudsman**
  Investigates the way complaints about a lawyer are dealt with by the lawyer's own professional body.
  www.olso.org

- **Scottish Legal Services Ombudsman**
  Investigates complaints about the way in which a professional body has handled a complaint against a legal practitioner.
  www.slso.org.uk

Mail order

- **Mail Order Traders' Association**
  Search whether a mail-order company is a member.
  www.adassoc.org.uk

- **Direct Marketing Association**
  Search whether a mail-order company is a member.
  www.dma.org.uk

- **National Newspaper Safe Home Ordering Protection Scheme (SHOPS)**
  Provides compensation to readers of national newspapers when the consumer buys directly from advertisements and catalogues inserted in national newspapers.
  www.shops-uk.org.uk

Unsolicited calls/mail/faxes

- **Mailing Preference Scheme**
  Removes your postal details from unwanted mailing lists.
  www.dma.org.uk

- **Telephone Preference Scheme**
  Enables consumers to opt out of receiving unsolicited sales and marketing calls.
  www.tpsonline.org.uk

- **Fax Preference Service**
  Enables consumers to opt out of receiving unsolicited sales and marketing faxes at home.
  www.fpsonline.org.uk

Office of Communications (OFCOM)

Ofcom is the regulator for the UK communications industry and it has responsibilities across television, radio, telecommunications and wireless communications services.
www.ofcom.org.uk

Press Complaints Commission (PCC)

The Press Complaints Commission (PCC) is an independent body which deals with complaints from members of the public about the editorial content of newspapers and magazines. Its service is free. For more information or to make a complaint, visit the website.
http://www.pcc.org.uk/

Water

- **Water Services Regulation Authority (Ofwat)**
  Ofwat is the economic regulator for the water and sewerage companies in England and Wales.
  www.ofwat.gov.uk

- **Consumer Council for Water**
  A national consumer watchdog agency for the water industry, complaints should go to your local water company in the first instance.
  www.ccwater.org.uk

- **Otelo (Telecommunications Ombudsman)**
  Deals with complaints related to Public Communication Providers.
  http://www.otelo.org.uk/

House-building and repairs, gas safety

- **Federation of Master Builders**
  http://www.fmb.org.uk/

- **National House-Building Council**
  Has a list of registered builders.
  http://www.nhbc.co.uk/

- **Gas Safe Register**
  Gas Safe Register became the official stamp for gas safety in Great Britain and the Isle of Man on 1 April 2009. CORGI gas registration is not valid or recognised by law in these regions. To work legally on gas appliances and installation, companies and engineers must be on the Gas Safe Register. Find registered traders and report illegal engineers on the website.
  www.gassaferegister.co.uk/

Other Useful Contacts

- **BBC – Consumer**
  http://www.bbc.co.uk/consumer/guides_to/

- **The UK Consumer Protection Agency**
  http://www.consumerprotectionagency.co.uk/

- **Which?**
  http://www.which.co.uk/

- **UK European Consumer Centre (ECC)**
  http://www.ukecc.net/

- **TrustMark**
  http://www.trustmark.org.uk/

- **How to Complain**
  http://www.howtocomplain.com/

- **Financial Services Authority**
  http://www.moneymadeclear.fsa.gov.uk/

- **Information Commissioner's Office**
  http://www.ico.gov.uk/

- **The Consumer Action Group**
  Online forum.
  http://www.consumeractiongroup.co.uk/forum/

- **How to contact your MP**
  http://www.upmystreet.com/commons/l/
  http://www.writetothem.com/
  http://www.theyworkforyou.com/mps/